Also by Martin Lloyd

The Passport
The Trouble with Spain
The Chinese Transfer
Every Picture
Hunting the Golden Lion
Rue Amélie
Neither Civil nor Servant
Fire, Smoke and Iron
The Impetus Turn

writing as K. T. Yalta
No Harm in Looking

The Trouble with France

Martin Lloyd

The Trouble with France

First published in 2004 by Queen Anne's Fan
PO Box 883 • Canterbury • Kent • CT1 3WJ

Reprinted 2005, 2006, 2008, 2009, 2010, this is getting silly, 2012, 2013, 2015, 2018

ISBN 9780 9547 1500 7

Martin Lloyd has recorded **The Trouble with France** as a talking book for the RNIB, catalogue number: TB15323

All characters and events portrayed in this book are absolutely true. Honest!   Any similarity to fiction of whatever sort is purely happenstantial and in the convoluted mind of the reader.

A complete catalogue record for this book can be obtained from the British Library on request.

A cross stitch pattern for the illustrations can be requested from the publishers if you really think it is worth it.

Cover photographs by Andrew Lloyd-Cook

Printed in England.

www.queenannesfan.com

Queen Anne's Fan

The Trouble with France . . .

The Trouble with France
THEATRE OF OPERATIONS

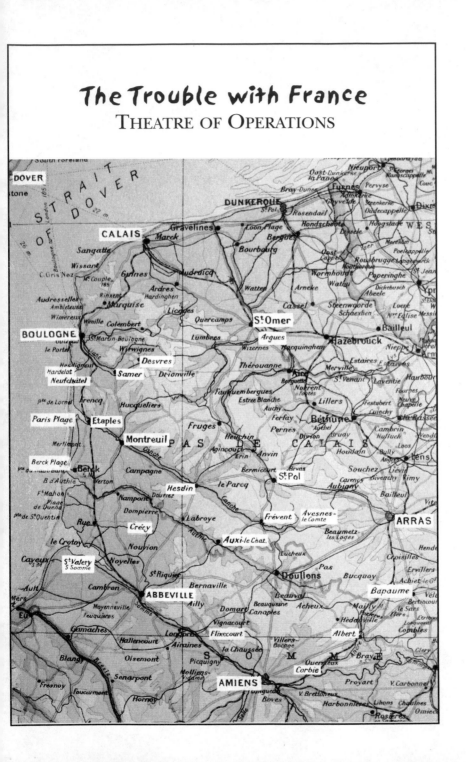

chapter one

'Crew announcement. Carpenter to the bridge please. Carpenter to the bridge.'

The sandy haired gentleman glanced up at the ship's tannoy. With a sinking feeling I saw him nod at the loudspeaker and then declare,

'Ah! The captain wants his coffee.'

Having opened the jaws of the mantrap he stood back to allow me to tread in it.

'But it was asking for the carpenter,' I protested.

He leaned forward. I could feel the jaws snapping around my ankle.

'Code.' He tapped the side of his blue-veined nose. 'It's all in code.'

'Code?' The more I wriggled the more tightly it seemed to grip.

'"Carpenter to the bridge" means that the captain wants his coffee.'

'But why don't they just say, "Can the captain have his coffee please?"'

He sucked in his breath with a hiss.

'Not good for the public image.'

This sounded silly to me.

'What do they say...' I asked, 'when they really want the carpenter?' Ha! Get out of that one! I thought.

'These cross-channel ferries don't have carpenters,' he declared, 'they are metal.' I gazed insolently at the wooden partitions by the duty free shop and the wooden counters in the self service restaurant. 'Well anyway,' he said, 'they don't call them "carpenters" anymore. They have some fancy title like "Marine Technician."' He looked at his watch. With all its levers and dials it looked just like the footplate of a miniature steam railway locomotive. 'We'll be in Boulogne in about half an hour.' He glanced at my cycling shorts. 'Are you going far?'

I do not hold myself responsible for the conversation that followed. It was perhaps unfortunate that unusual circumstances had precipitated my presence on board this ferry and possibly I did just enjoy being a teeny bit obtuse, but all that I told him was true.

'Well, Frank and I decided to go touring on our bikes in Suffolk.'

'Suffolk?'

'Yes, I've never been to Suffolk and Frank said that it was nice so we decided to go there.'

He looked through the salty window where the English Channel was steadily streaming past in a jumble of green foam and hovercraft.

'What are you doing on this boat then?'

'Ah well, you see we live in Kent and if you want to get to Suffolk by bike then you have to cross the Thames and this means that you have to practically cycle into London and out again so I looked at the map and decided that the most sensible way was to go by boat.'

'To Suffolk?'

This was now the second time that he had pronounced

the word 'Suffolk' and I could not help but detect a certain tinge of incredulity slipping into his enunciation.

'I know a friend in the ticket office,' I confided, but that did not seem to help him. 'He worked out our route for us. We pop over to Zeebrugge from Dover on the early morning boat, change boats in Zeebrugge and take the afternoon boat back to Felixstowe. Quite clever eh? Kent to Suffolk via Belgium and you get duty-frees as well.' I sat back, proud of myself but something seemed to be niggling him. He glanced at Cap Gris Nez lying on the port side.

'But er...' he began and then looked into the bottom of his glass. A slice of lemon stared back at him in a watery demi-lunar grin. He opened his mouth and then closed it and looked again at the coast of France. Finally he could restrain himself no longer.

'But this boat is going to Boulogne, not Zeebrugge.'

'Oh I know. That doesn't matter. I can't go to Suffolk anyway. Frank rolled his car two days ago and can't afford to come so I cashed in the tickets and chose to go to France instead.'

'So you're not going to Suffolk then?'

Isn't it strange how people can latch onto one thing?

Unknown to me, that innocuous conversation marked the beginning of a relationship between me and France which was to develop over the following years into an obsessive battle. Wherever I went in France and whatever I tried to do, nothing turned out as it should have done. Straightforward tasks became operations of indescribable complexity and even simple conversations turned into dialogues of the surreal. It took me some time to face up to the truth that a sinister curse had been cast upon me. France had never forgiven me for putting it second on my list after Suffolk. The irony is that even to this day, I have still never been to Suffolk but trying to explain that to France is as fruitless as arguing with a vending machine.

So, carefree and excited, I bumped over the polished iron molehills in the car-deck and slithered down the wet steel mesh ramp onto the soil of France. I had a bike and a map and a pocket full of francs. What more could I need? Within three hundred yards of the dock gate I discovered that I needed a cycle mechanic. Fifteen love! France was not wasting any time.

Behind the bus station I discovered a cycle shop. That is to say, I assumed it to be a cycle shop for although its grimy windows were festooned with all the recognisable and many of the less familiar parts of bicycles, there appeared not to be one complete and assembled machine inside.

I bounced in and cracked my head on a wheel which had been hanging on a wire from the ceiling. After the impact it fell to the counter and in one bound, landed on a cardboard tray displaying light bulbs. These it catapulted, somersaulting, into the diagonal corner of the crowded shop, rattling and tinkling gaily as they showered down through naked spoked wheels and rolled into inaccessible corners. I lunged forwards to stop the wheel in its pogo stick-like excursion but I found myself arrested around the midriff because a pedal crank mounted on a sales board behind me had inserted itself into the back pocket of my shorts.

'Don't move.' I had heard that said in so many cowboy films that I found it incongruous on the lips of the blank-faced French woman standing behind the counter. 'Don't move!' she ordered as her thumb slid along the edge of the counter and her fingers reached for the button secreted underneath.

She was small and was lashed into a floral apron like a lump of heavy machinery on the exposed well-deck of a North Atlantic cargo ship. We looked at each other and I could tell from the whitening of her thumb that she was pressing that buzzer for all she was worth. Behind her, dirty wooden pigeonholes climbed to the grimy ceiling. They housed more obscure parts of bicycles and some tins and wooden boxes bearing ancient trade illustrations.

She shifted her glance to a man who was crossing the alleyway towards the shop.

'My husband,' she divulged.

Her husband was no taller than she and passed under the stalactites of cycle wheels and frames without disturbing a white hair of his head.

'Monsieur?' he piped in the conventional intonation of commerce.

Forgetting that the giant presentation of cranks and chainwheels was still attached to me, I made a step forwards and began to explain my problem. His eyes jerked in alarm to a spot above and behind my head as the eight foot high display board heaved itself languidly from the wall like a bouncer in a nightclub. He scurried behind the counter and stood next to his wife. Whether this was in order to protect her or save himself, I was not sure.

I detached myself from the pyramid which sank back into place, doubtless to plan its next ambush. With some approximate French and accurate gesticulation, I told him the problem. The chain was jumping and cracking over the gears on the back wheel.

He wheeled my machine across the alleyway to his motorcycle shop. Standing alongside the nobbly-tyred, oil smelling gargantuae, my bicycle looked very frail and vulnerable and I began to doubt whether it would survive for the five days of my proposed trip.

Producing a screwdriver from a secret fold of his overalls, he quickly adjusted the derailleur mechanism to a nicety. The problem ceased to exist.

He would not take my money. He insisted that he had made no repair, only an adjustment and that it had hardly taken any of his time. I thanked him, opened the door and sent tottering a motocyclette with only one wheel.

Together we watched it, writhing this way and that as it made vain attempts to regain its balance. Then it abruptly gave up the struggle and sat like a Buddha on the concrete floor. The man shrugged and indicated that the doorway was now clear. I smiled and left.

As I passed by the cycle shop I looked for madame to bid her thanks but she was on her hands and knees, coaxing light bulbs out from under the counter with the handle of a broom and so I left her to her snooker. All in all, I thought that I had acquitted myself quite well.

When it comes to the needs of tourists, Calais and Boulogne share a common transparency with Dover and Folkestone. 'How do I get to the Prisunic?' translates as '*Ou est Marks et Sparks?*' and 'Where is the road to Paris?' becomes '*C'est bon pour Londres?*' The visitor to these towns only recognises two options – either you stock up with essentials or you try to get straight through without touching the sides. And yet, surely these four ports are steeped in history? They are, and it is one which clearly establishes the origins for today's dichotomy, because, for several millennia, foreigners either plundered the towns or landed in order to belt inland and invade somewhere more important.

Now take Boulogne for instance, and let's face it, through the years many people have. It was a Roman port, has been and still is an important fishing port, it has a fortified citadel and, until the Canadians replanned the town in 1944, had many other fine buildings. It also has a sense of ridicule. The slightly daft Roman emperor Caligula, he who allegedly appointed his horse as a Consul, came here in 40AD and raised a legion or two to invade England. He set out and once out of sight of land, promptly turned back to Boulogne. Leaving his troops with the commission of building a triumphal tower overlooking the town, he filled his pockets with shells gathered from the beach and then beetled off back to Rome where he was received in triumph. Well, qualified triumph, since he was assassinated the following year. But the tower his soldiers built was used as a lighthouse until it was pulled down in the seventeenth century. Probably as a result of some central government cost-cutting measures.

And what about King Edward the Confessor's brother in law, Eustace of Boulogne? He visited England in 1051 but had a bit of trouble on his return journey. Whilst waiting for a ship, he decided to quarter himself and his men in the town of Dover. This was not a case of his graciously accepting the town's invitation to partake of its hospitality; it was Eustace authorising his men to take what they wanted unbidden. Indeed, when they had been but a few miles from Dover they had stopped to put on their mail suits.

Not surprisingly the Dovorians did not agree with this behaviour and some went as far as to resist. What started as a simple dispute ended in a bloodletting with about twenty persons killed on both sides. Eustace then withdrew the remainder of his men inland and he was probably lucky to have escaped with his life.

The two Napoleons left their mark on Boulogne, one way or another. Bonaparte had a dock basin constructed in 1801 to shelter some of the two thousand ships he had collected for his planned invasion of England. The invasion never took place but the dock is still there, just the other side of the quay at which the Folkestone boat unloads.

And in 1840, Prince Louis Napoleon, he who was to become Napoleon III, landed at Boulogne in his second ill-judged attempt at insurrection against the rule of King Louis Philippe.

By the beginning of the twentieth century, Boulogne was a fashionable seaside resort with a casino and seafront hotels hiring out hundreds of bathing machines. The port not only received the cross-channel packets from Dover, Folkestone, and Ramsgate but also the steamers from

London, Goole and Hull. Coastwise to France it had services to La Rochelle, Le Havre, St Nazaire, Bordeaux and Bayonne. But most surprising is the number of high seas vessels which ran from Boulogne. Perusing the docks and quays today, one can only marvel at what must have been the diminutive size of the ships which sailed the oceans to New York, Montevideo, Rio de Janeiro, Las Palmas, Lagos and Conakry.

Two statistical facts from this period bear consideration: one hundred years ago the population of Boulogne town was five percent English and the crossing time from Folkestone to Boulogne was an hour and twenty minutes. The English population is now just two percent and the crossing, an hour and fifty minutes. The obvious deduction is that the mathematical formula is an inverse ratio: the more English you have in your population the less minutes it takes the ships to cross the Channel.

What was I to be – a plunderer or invader? A bit of both. By four o'clock in the afternoon I was about ten miles inland and regretting my hurried purchase of *pain au chocolat* and *chausson aux pommes* in lieu of lunch. Not for their quality but their quantity. I was hungry.

Over on my distant right, a sinister wood climbed the escarpment, hemming in my road. On my left, a flat bottomed valley accommodated a stream and a sprinkling of farms. I looked at my map. It was as it should be. Behind me was Samer, whose town centre was revetted in a chaos of pavé which resembled a retirement home for worn-out staircases. Crossing the square on my bicycle had left an impression on me which was to take several days to wear off. On the outskirts of the town I had cycled past the modern factory of Blanzy whose ancestors in Boulogne had turned out four million gross steel pen nibs per annum to make Boulogne the nib centre of France. Now before me, according to my map, was Desvres, famous in the region for its faience. Here, I would stop for the night. Desvres would have a hotel, a restaurant and perhaps a little nocturnal animation to distract me before I slipped between the sheets.

It was in Desvres that for the first and what will probably be the only time in my life, I discovered a topographical feature which corresponded exactly to its symbol on the map. You know the problem; the map tells you that the church is a black dot with a cross on top and when you enter the village you find it is a red brick belfry grafted onto a rectangular stone nave. There is no feature in the village which in any way could be described as a black dot surmounted by a cross.

So, I was making for the railway station, guessing that I would find there an underpriced and practically empty hotel. I stopped at the corner of the street and unfolded my map. Now, that yellow line is the road which I am on at the moment, that patch of green is the orchard on my right and this empty white rectangle must be....

My view to the left was blocked by a brick wall so I leaned my bicycle against a pole and crossed over. It was silly really. I did not need to see what was behind the wall. I was certain that I was on the correct road but something urged me to check. I looked over the top. It was just like the map said – an empty white rectangle. It had been a cement works but it had been razed to the concrete foundations. Only a blank, white rectangle remained.

I felt as though an elaborate hoax had been played upon me. I wondered if Desvres had furnished the inspiration for the design of the cartographic symbols of the *Institut Géographique National.* Perhaps the town was full of houses shaded with grey diagonal lines, marshy areas liberally sprinkled with those three-black-spike-and-one-across plants, and hills with brown lines running around them to tell you how high they were.

It wasn't.

I grasped the massive handle and pushed the iron and glass door of the Hotel de la Gare. It was heavy and because of this I probably applied more effort than I should have done. Once I had started the door moving I was faced with the problem of trying to stop it as it swung inwards, accelerating all the time, dragging me inexorably with it. It crashed against the rubber stop and rebounded. I had understood more about the concepts of momentum and inertia in the space of the last four seconds than my physics master had been able to teach me in four years.

Like an animated eiderdown of tan and white, a dog slowly hauled itself up from the tiled floor and padded arthritically over towards me. Its golden eyes were tinged with ginger eyelashes. It sniffed at my ankles and then growled. A woman called, *'Couche-toi!'* from the other end of the bar and the dog wandered diffidently away and collapsed like some pneumatic contraption that had been punctured, wheezing and hissing as its limbs nobbled onto the cold floor.

I moved into the echoing bar of the hotel. At one end, young men in spats and young ladies with parasols were alighting from the Paris express. They smiled freshly down at me from the ceramic mural in which they had been fixed one hundred years before. The silvering was peeling from the backs of the musty mirrors, which showed a muslin reflection of the dusty chandeliers and the wrought iron and marble tables.

Against the bar leaned a French workman in dumpy blue overalls. A yellow cigarette hung in his mouth. On the zinc bar top his latest glass of wine stood untouched. He was leaning across the zinc to ensure the confidentiality of his conversation despite there being no other customers. Listening intently, with one hand plunged into the sink was a young lady of striking appearance. Her jet black hair hung in long hanks, her eyes were dark glass marbles set in deep sockets. Her skin was pale and she wore a black blouse and skirt. You won't believe this bit, but I swear that it is true. On her shoulder sat a raven.

'Monsieur?'

'Do you have a room for me for tonight please?'

'I regret monsieur, we don't 'do' hotel anymore.'

'Is there another hotel?'

She looked at the workman. I looked at the raven. They both twitched their heads, though probably for different reasons.

'Baa.... What's his name, up there,' he suggested. The workman, that is, not the raven.

'Yes, up on the main road, at the crossroads,' the lady translated for me.

Later that night I was to bitterly regret not having asked the raven.

At the fag end of the town I found the miserable café-bar-hotel crouching in the lee of three roads, none of which seemed to want to be associated with its mean corner doorway and shuttered windows. I was discouraged but tried to reassure myself by remarking that above the door was painted the legend *Hotel*. But then, I could have made the same observation at the Hotel de la Gare and that had sported a raven in the bar. I went in.

'I won't do dinner,' she warned me.

'No, that's fine thank you.'

'Just the bed.'

'Yes, I understand. How much?'

She shrewdly eyed my dusty legs and spiky hair.

'Forty five francs for the bed,' she declared, convinced that this would send me on my way.

'Splendid! Shall I pay now?'

'Pay me in the morning. But I don't do dinner.' She watched her final shot splash short of the target.

We don't do hotel anymore. I won't do dinner. The town

did not seem to 'do' anything at all. On my way from the station I had gone into a patisserie to buy a snack but nobody had come to serve me so I had stolen out again, fearful that I should have been caught leaving and been suspected of evil intent.

Opposite the shop, with the dogged inflexibility of ceramic tiles, gold and green art deco letters had insisted that the hairdresser's was really a horsemeat butcher's. All around the square, the newer businesses had ousted the old but behind and around the cheap plastic fascias the obdurate tiles stubbornly proclaimed their original devotions and denied the identity of the usurpers.

Her son showed me where I could lean my bicycle against a wall in the triangular yard. He jerked his head towards a stable door which was fixed closed by a short length of grubby string.

'Les waters.'

My nose had already reached that conclusion. The boy returned to the bar, plugged himself into a pinball machine and began to writhe and jerk in sensual agony before it.

I decided to dine out. It was 6.30 and the town was shut. I trudged on, trying to convince myself that there, just around the corner, I would discover a gaily lit street, half way down which there would nestle one of those restaurants that forever after would be remembered for being as great a discovery as the Victoria Falls. But there was not and worse still, there was no-one in the street of whom I could enquire. It was as if the town were under a curfew.

At last I came across a homeless soul, or a curfew breaker, who after listening with deepening gloom to my enquiry opined that there might still, perhaps, be... indeed, (with a little vehemence) it was the only place where one could eat and it was 'up on the main road'. I followed his directions, past cold, empty shops, down dark, deserted, echoing streets till I was afforded a new vista on my café-bar-hotel where I knew they 'won't do dinner'.

I sprinted half a mile down the main road towards a glowing supermarket sign. I managed to get in before the trolleys were chained up for the night and out before the covers went over the tills.

Back in the café-bar-hotel I tried to be sociable and sipped a hot chocolate. It was difficult as I was the only customer. The bar exuded the welcoming ambiance of a dentist's waiting room. With exaggerated disregard, I tossed my plastic supermarket bag onto the bench and then winced at the sound that two tins of sardines, four bread rolls and a bar of chocolate make when they hit a wooden board. To be caught eating in a hotel room in France is a capital offence nearly as heinous as putting ice cubes in the wine.

I was the only customer in the bar. What on earth did the commerce live on? Surely not the passing trade for it seemed to do just that – pass. I watched madame. Her blonde hair was showing black at the roots and the bags under her eyes were deepening by the minute. Then the police arrived. Or to be exact, *a* police arrived. Was this the husband? Not judging by the way that he was greeted with resigned sufferance.

The woman left the bar and they huddled all three in the corner under the staircase, mumbling together. From time to time one or other or all three would glance across at me. Were they afraid that I could hear what they were saying? I thought of the blue workman in the Hotel de la Gare, leaning across the bar to talk to the barlady. Were they talking about me? Had they all heard the clink of the sardine tins? Were they awaiting the perpetration of my crime? I could imagine the discussion...

'Wait till he goes up and then Pierre can nip up and listen outside his door.'

'And when he hears the sardine tin being opened–'

'I'll rush in with the handcuffs!'

The following morning, the sun was shining; the coffee strong and scalding; the bread, fresh and crispy and the jam, home-made. Madame greeted me with a jaunty, 'Good morning. Did you sleep well?' and her son asked a couple of healthily pertinent questions about my bicycle. Even as I pushed off from the kerb, the gendarme alighted from his 4L and wished me, *'Bonne route!'*

And all that for forty five francs. What a rich dividend for such a poor town!

chapter two

I don't know what you think of guide books but I have to take most of what they say with a pinch of salt and I would not trust travel writers further than I could throw their egos. They always manage to see the best sights and eat the best meals and undergo the funniest experiences where nomal people such as you and I would have eaten a cheese sandwich whilst sitting in the pouring rain on the wall outside the abattoir and would have been silly enough to have said so.

How do they do it? Are they so marvellously clever at predicting interesting occurrences? Are they really such percipient observers and knowledgable interpreters or... do they make it up?

I'll give you a frinstance. Have you ever been to the Mont St. Michel in Brittany? Almost anybody can tell you it is a fortified prominence almost surrounded by the sea and linked to the mainland by a causeway which you can walk along at low tide. When the tide recedes, the water disappears out of the bay, leaving the Mount stranded on the sand flats.

Almost in the same breath your enthusiast will go on to say that when the tide comes in, the breakers tumble over themselves like matrons at the January sales and surround and isolate the Mount so quickly that, and mark these words, because they will be the ones he will use, 'a man on a galloping horse is unable to outpace them'. He says all this because it is written in the guidebook.

If you press your friend closer he might feel obliged to insist that he has seen it although he will add that he was disappointed that the standard equine yardstick was not available for comparison.

It may be what he wanted to see; it may be what he wants you to believe he has seen, but he did not see it because it does not happen. The sea oozes in at a leisurely amble and sidles around the fringes of the bay in the same way that a group of tourists will shuffle around the walls of a crypt whilst awaiting the guide to start talking. You would have enough time to pack up and carry off your deck chairs and not have to lash them frantically together like a raft and ride ashore on the twelve foot high surf wave.

I know because I have been there. I went there on the day of the highest tide of the twentieth century and the sea only just managed to cross the causeway. So when slight acquaintances relate graphic accounts of hordes of white-eyed cavalry thundering across the bay, the steeds flecked with foam and the riders slashing them madly with their crops whilst the might of the Atlantic Ocean rolls on behind like Time's winged chariot at their heels, I merely smile patronisingly. It infuriates them.

I mention all this because when I arrived at Montreuil its road sign insisted that the town was called, 'Montreuil-sur-mer' despite compelling and widespread proof to suggest the contrary. This evidence took the form of rolling green meadows and fluffy white sheep on a 360 degree azimuth.

Nervously eyeing the valley for foam-flecked horsemen, I prepared myself for a preposterous explanation. None was forthcoming. Even the *syndicat d'initiative* which can usually produce some pearls was remarkably barren. The girl there shrugged her shoulders.

I walked around the ramparts as all good tourists should do. I had started off by trying to cycle along them (which no good tourist should do) until I realised that the shrubs poking above the edge of the verge were in fact, the tops of forty-foot trees and that there was nothing to stop me from hurtling off into space.

Had I read *Les Misérables* by Victor Hugo I would no doubt have imagined Jean Valjean stomping through the town and had I paid attention at school I might have felt the loneliness of General Haig in his HQ, making terrible decisions here during the Great War, but I had done neither. When I got home, of course, my friends made it plain that I was the only person in Britain who could be so insensitive to the evidence of the past but for now I looked at the town with eyes uncorrupted by history or literature.

I fetched up in a square and decided to do some sketching. Modest though I am, I can honestly say that I am a bit of a dab hand with the jolly old pen and ink. A flourish here, some cross-hatching there and *voilà*, another masterpiece of technical understatement.

Seated there with my bicycle leaning against the back of my bench and sheltered from the heat by the wafting plane trees, I looked around for a challenge. Something to stretch me. The trees were fairly uninspiring, the pétanque players, disobligingly, would not stand still. The obvious answer was the fountain. Not for the beauty of it but because I could not properly see it. The sun was shining directly into my eyes and the central core of the fountain was a writhing black silhouette, painful to behold. Its shape was a nonsense of ridiculous angles and disjointed curves. An amorphous amphigouri. This would be a real challenge.

I chose my thick pen, screwed up my eyes like a cigarette smoker and set to work with a purpose. I find that it helps to frown every now and then otherwise people don't take you seriously. After ten minutes of inking and about five of frowning, any casual observer could have seen that I was succeeding uncannily in transferring to my pad the form of the shapeless blob.

As luck would have it, I was observed. One of the more curious and, no doubt, patrician, boule players had wandered across with his hands in his pockets and now stood respectfully behind my bench so as not to block my view. I always work better with an audience. I put on a really awe-inspiring frown and then added another blob.

My observer followed my gaze and imitated my frown and then surpassed it. He pushed up the rim of his beret with his thumb. He looked to the right, to the left, behind him, up in the air, down on the ground and each time his gaze returned to my pad and his face contorted in a frown.

'*On dirait un baton de réglisse,*' he observed at last and then ambled away, whistling with his cigarette still in his mouth, which is no mean feat. It was not until the following day that I found someone who could tell me what the translation of, '*on dirait un baton de réglisse*' was.

'It looks like a stick of liquorice.'

I think that man was very rude.

This part of Northern France is characterised by three parallel river valleys running roughly south east to north west. Nearest to Boulogne is the valley of the river Canche which runs around the foot of Montreuil and reaches the sea between Etaples and Le Touquet. South of this is the Authie which wriggles its way into a secret, remote, mud filled bay just below Berck and further down, the geriatric Somme staggers out and collapses in full view of a small town with the unappetising name of Le Crotoy.

I decided to stay the night at Hesdin, a town further up the northernmost valley, that of the river Canche. As I left

Montreuil behind me, I knew that I had made a correct decision. The valley was green and luscious and the Canche wandered across it, visiting lakes and pools and rippling under the poplar trees as it made its unconcerned way down to the sea behind me.

Into this verdant tableau surged a garish intruder which, whenever it appears, despite its chromatic incongruity, always represents for me the very distillation of the French countryside – a stuttering, red and cream diesel railcar. You only see them in the country. Like policemen on bicycles and children with baskets. This one snuffled and growled along the bottom of the valley as it played hopscotch with the river.

I arrived in Hesdin earlier than I had anticipated and so I occupied my time by looking for a hotel. This achieved, I would be able to visit the town with my mind at complete rest. I could not have foreseen how the day was going to end and how far from that desired rest my mind would be.

There were three hotels in Hesdin. One was closed, another very expensive and the third was thus, exactly what I was looking for. It was a small but tall hotel opposite the station. I parked my bicycle carefully outside and entered the bar. Inside was all noise and brouhaha. A lad of about twenty years confirmed willingly that they had a room but that it would not be ready until five o'clock.

'Can I eat here?' I asked.

'Yes, you can. Tonight we are doing a mussels and chips evening.'

He had to shout to make himself heard above the cacophony of the juke box and he used the familiar *tu* form of the verb. I resented this because I had learned at school that one only used the *tu* form to strangers if they were children, pets or lunatics and I wondered under which classification he had placed me.

'There will be lots of people here tonight,' he shouted. 'It is very popular.'

Well, I didn't mind that. It would do me good to mix with the populace a little. I had already discovered that the trouble with solo cycling was that you only had yourself to talk to and most of the time you knew what you were going to say next. A knees-up with the peasants whilst scoffing plates full of mussels and chips would do me the world of good. It would be a contrast to my solitary night in Desvres.

'Céline!' he yelled at a short girl who was standing about two feet distant from him. 'This bloke wants a room for tonight.' He nodded in my direction. 'I've given him number eight and told him to come back at five.'

Céline made no sign of having understood or even of having heard what had been said to her but this did not appear to bother either of the participants in the exercise.

'I will ask you to stick your name in the register.' He handed me an open ledger and explained the blank sheet. 'We've only just started at the hotel.'

A register! I had not seen a hotel register in France for fifteen years. I thought that they had been thrown away with the police forms. I was a little ruffled. Firstly by his dogged persistence in addressing me in the most familiar fashion despite my scorching glances of disapproval and secondly by being referred to as 'this bloke'. I eschewed his chewed ball-point and flourished my fountain. In my best copperplate I carefully wrote, *'Michael Mouse, occupation: rodent'* across the two columns. Well, I thought it was witty.

He showed me the gate at the back of the hotel and told me that when I returned at five o'clock I could put my bicycle in the garage there. I went off to explore.

I rode around the town a couple of times and realised that what I wanted to do was sit on a bench in the sun and watch the world go by, so I did just that. With a selfish disregard for the requirements of the tourist, the world stopped going by after three quarters of an hour and Hesdin sunk into a heavy torpor. I perused my map to pass the time, mentally exploring the exits from the town ready for the continuation of my journey on the morrow. Little did I know how soon I was to use that information.

At five o'clock the town rolled over and settled on the other pillow. I wobbled to a halt outside the hotel and the boy waved me around to the side gate.

'Max! Shut yer big gob!' he shouted at a mangy alsatian which circled around as I pushed my bike into the open garage. He squeaked the wrought iron gates back together, leaving the padlock dangling from its hasp. I took out my cycle lock. Even if he did not care if somebody stole his gates, I would lock my bike.

'When you're ready, come in there.' He pointed to the door. 'Through the kitchen and into the bar.'

I was not worried about entering a hotel by the back door but I had learned many moons ago never to look into the kitchen if I intended eating at the establishment. I was not interested in the many obscure processes involved in making the raw material ready for consumption, just the end product.

The kitchen was exactly like the kitchen in almost any old French house. A cast-iron range, high ceilings, pots and pans, red and white check table in the middle and red and purple knitted grandma slumped on a chair in the corner. I said 'bonjour' to her but she did not respond. Possibly she was unable to hear me above the wall-bulging, floor-thumping beat of the juke box. I smiled to myself. If they thought that a little bit of noise like that would stop me from sleeping then they had obviously not heard of my fantastic powers of concentration and relaxation.

The young man flung open the door and thrust a key into the hand which I had desperately thrown up to protect myself from what I had erroneously assumed to be an unprovoked attack. He nodded silently towards a sombre staircase which I had not noticed and slammed the door again, just like a cuckoo clock

I grappled with my bags as best as I could and waddled

27

up the staircase towards the yellow light of the afternoon sun as it filtered into the corridor and landing above me.

Room six, room seven, here we are, room eight. The door was open for me but I stopped on the threshold, transfixed by the sight. Down the middle of the unmade bed, the sheets were twisted in a sordid corkscrew. On the grey pillow squatted a Vesuvius of cigarette ash which had spilled from the vulgar cut glass ashtray. A china cup lay on its side on the floor and the bottom of the curtain hung sodden, into the sink.

I knew immediately that there was now no way they could convincingly prepare this room for me. It was already etched in my memory. Indeed it makes me shudder to describe it. I resolved to give them the benefit of the doubt. Never be too hasty. I waited, in case I had been given the wrong room. Nobody came. Below me, the floor heaved and breathed the rank irresponsibility of youth. So they had just taken over this hotel, had they? Their enterprise would surely fail and they would blame it on anything and everything apart from their suicidal disregard for the respect and comfort of their potential customers.

I felt better after that pontificating and made up my mind that I would walk out and go elsewhere. I had no desire to cause a scene in the bar, there were far too many of them to hope for a useful discussion, so I chose the quick exit through the kitchens. Unnoticed by me, the Curse of France swung smoothly into operation.

Arriving at the foot of the stairs, I grasped the knob of the kitchen door and pulled it towards me. I was left stupidly holding the door handle as it came off, attached to a long spike. Simultaneously, from the other side of the door came a sequence of noises which could only have been caused by a porcelain door knob dropping from a door and rolling across a tiled kitchen floor.

Panic! I dropped my cycle bags, squatted down and tried to espy daylight through the spindle hole. My proddings became less accurate and more frantic as I hurried, urged on by an irrational terror of being discovered trying to sneak away from a hotel which could not provide its guests with clean rooms. At last I made contact and the door grated open, flooding the cubbyhole with light.

It was possibly being dazzled by this light which caused me to overlook the copper plate which had been propped up to dry on the range. As I swung up my bags I caught it a blow and launched it on a balletic trajectory which took it across the kitchen floor, emulating a Viennese Waltz even to the final nerve-shattering spin and curtsey. Encumbered by my bags, I lumbered forwards to intercept it on one of its swoops but only succeeded in kicking the doorknob neatly under the huge Breton dresser.

Now, at this point I should have recognised who was winning and simply conceded the game but I must have been spurred on by a misconceived feeling of guilt. Misconceived, because it would have been patently obvious to any impartial bystander that none of this was my fault.

From her chair in the corner, the purple and red knitted grandma watched me silently. I had to make amends of some sort. I could not crawl under the dresser to retrieve the doorknob so I picked up the plate. It seemed the least that I could do.

Had I thought longer, I suppose I would have realised that a copper plate which had been reclining on a roaring kitchen range for two hours would be hot, but I didn't. It took me about a second to learn my mistake by which time the plate was at hip height. With a yelp I released it into the beckoning arms of gravity. And with a single-mindedness which looked suspiciously like premeditation, it made straight for the corner and knocked over four of the six empty wine bottles which immediately rolled into the starburst display which has since been used to great effect by the Red Arrows. That was enough for me. I gathered my bags around me and, hopping over the parabolic peregrinations of the dispersing bottles, I left the hotel via the door into the yard.

I don't dislike dogs, but I often find them infuriatingly stupid. Consider Max the mangy alsatian for example; resident of the hotel, guard dog, he must have known that the door from the kitchen opened outwards into the yard so why the devil had he stretched himself out full length upon the step? This kind of senseless behaviour, whether done for amusement or a dare, only serves to reinforce the belief in the minds of the cynics, that a dog is the one animal which can surpass man for stupidity.

The door caught him a blow in the scrawny ribs and then bounced back into my face, smiting me gratuitously across the cheek in biblical fashion. Max grumbled, although I cannot for the life of me see why. Whilst I entreated him to maintain a discreet profile in order to allow me to slink across the yard, he defied me gaily with a flamboyant demonstration of barking, yelping, growling, snarling and ridiculous little jumps quite unbecoming to a dog with any self esteem.

Cursing him under my breath, I reached the garage which was concealed from the rear of the hotel. I feverishly strapped my bags onto the bike whilst Max watered the rusty wheels of a beige Mercedes. My strategic withdrawal was becoming a rout.

'Come and play with me,' said Max. I ignored him and pushed my bike out towards the gate. 'Come and see what I have got,' he insisted.

'Some other time Max, I must go.'

'I think you should look at what I've got. Growl, growl.'

'Max, I have got better things to do than... Max, give me back my map.'

'Come and play with me.'

'This is not funny, Max. I need that map.'

'I'm pretending that it is a rat. Look, growl, growl, wrench, shake.'

'DON'T DO THAT! Alright, I'm sorry I shouted. Please can I have my map?'

'I can throw it up in the air like this and it gets bigger. Grrrr. This is fun isn't it?'

'Max! Look er... Come this way. Away from the kitchen.'

'I'm gonna show grandma my rat.'

'Max! Here boy! Come and have a game. Come on.'

'Yipee! I knew you'd play. Oi, let go of my collar.'

'I bet you can't bark.'

'Just watch me. Woof!'

'Thank you, now buzz off.'

''Ere, you've got my rat. I'm gonna tell grandma of you.'

He pounded off to the kitchen door and I ran with my bike in the opposite direction. Thank goodness the gate had not been locked. As I passed through I heard voices and the slamming of a door. In a flash of mischievous inspiration, I snapped the padlock shut.

I dared not risk cycling across the front of the hotel so I turned sharp left and wound my bicycle up to top speed. Around by the industrial alcohol distillery I sped, tyres singing on soft tar. This was exhilarating. Riding a loaded bicycle, fast through the streets called for a physical stamina and mental agility that I knew I did not possess and I expected that it would only be a matter of time before the law of probability caught up with me and I came a cropper.

As I heaved my bicycle through a chicane of parked cars, I caught sight of a reflection in the shop window ahead. It was of a beige Mercedes with rusty wheels, jumping from shop to shop, a different shape each time. But where was it? I braked hard, feeling the momentum of my loaded bags urging the bike onwards. As soon as I had got it under control I lurched off down a sudden alleyway.

It brought me quickly to the other street and, looking around the corner like a cowboy in Dodge City, I glimpsed the tail of the Mercedes as it turned into the street that I had just vacated. They were taking a quick look around the block and I had nearly met them halfway! I pushed straight across the street and disappeared into the alley opposite. I lost track of direction, right, left, right, left. Suddenly I saw a sign, *'Frévent'*. I had the map fresh in my mind and without a moment's hesitation I swerved off, leaving Hesdin and my hotel for the night.

I rode on to Frévent. It was the next town. I had nowhere else to go. My legs were like lead. I went slower and slower. At half past eight I was standing exhausted but triumphant outside the only hotel in the town.

Two minutes later I was back on the pavement again. Shattered. This was not what I had come to France for. This was not carefree cycling. In desolation I sat on the kerb outside and put my head in my hands. I could go no further. If they had no room for me here then I would sleep outside on the pavement.

chapter three

So much for French hospitality! I had only asked for a room. One measly room. You can't tell me that they are completely full.

'Monsieur!'

I suppose if I had rolled up in a posh car and waved a credit card, everything would have been different.

'Monsieur!'

Just because I am on a cycle and look as if I need a wash they are not interested. Well, I've had just about enough of France and the French and their lousy–

'MONSIEUR!'

'Yes?'

'We have a room. One we had overlooked.'

'Oh thank you, thank you very much.'

'No, don't leave your bike outside, someone might steal it, bring it into the bar.'

'But it's dirty.'

'Oh, not very. We wash the floor every morning after breakfast. It was lucky that you didn't go far away. My sister said to me, "What about Ernest's room?" Of course I had forgotten all about it.'

'Well thank you.'

'I suppose you have eaten already? We don't open the restaurant in the evening. Just lunches at midday for the workmen.'

'Yes, I've... I've eaten already,' I lied.

The indecision showed in her eyes as she handed me the key. My fingers closed around it luxuriously. Even a broom cupboard was more than I could have hoped for on that night.

I was up in the roof on the fourth floor. From the window I could trace my route up the valley from Hesdin. I would never forget it.

Although I was hungry, I was sure that my weariness would overcome any complaints from my stomach. I washed meticulously at the sink, indulging lavish attention upon my toes as I dried them. 'This little cochon....'

I thought of the two sisters downstairs, wringing their hands in anxiety as they told me that they were full. Had they really forgotten this room or had it been the sight of me slumped dejectedly at the side of my bike that had changed their minds? How uncharitable I was being! Someone knocked at the door. I arranged myself decently and opened it.

'Madame says that you should eat before sleeping.' On the plate was a succulent ham sandwich. I gazed at it, not daring to blink in case it disappeared.

'Convey my thanks to Madame,' I said at last and took the plate from her.

She tossed her auburn hair and as she smoothed her

hands sensually down her shirt she said, 'Is there anything else that I can do for you?'

'I have everything I need thank you. Goodnight.'

I shut the door, wolfed down the sandwich and was asleep within minutes.

Nine o'clock in the morning and I awoke with a start. What had she said? I recalled her hands as they had moved over her splendid torso. What had she said? What had she meant? Who was she? Had I dreamt her? No, she had been real, there was the plate with the sandwich crumbs on. Would you believe how dense I could be? I just said 'Goodnight' and went to sleep didn't I?

I cleaned my teeth so savagely that I almost bit the end from my toothbrush. How could I ever live this down? I mean, she had been pretty obvious hadn't she? I pulled my clothes on roughly, still angry with myself. Then I calmed down. Suddenly, I knew what I should do to preserve my reputation. I would tell nobody. I would keep her a secret. And that's what I did.

All that day I cycled to Arras. It was a pleasant enough day and the countryside, although undulating, was not taxing. Reliving the events of the previous day I laughed out aloud as I imagined the rusty wheeled Mercedes still charging around Hesdin looking for a Michael Mouse. How clever I was!

At the side of the road appeared a monumental brick and stone gateway and as I had nothing better to do, I stopped. I had seen the distinctive green and white metal direction signs in several places before but had never bothered to investigate. It was not really the kind of thing that attracted me.

Commonwealth War Graves Commission.
Duisans British Cemetery.

It was cool under the gateway so I sat on the stone bench

in the shade and ate my picnic. I cleared up and returned to my bike. It seemed a bit mean just to use the gateway as a picnic site and not visit the cemetery, but cemeteries do not interest me.

I come from one of those families which has been untouched by all wars. We have no tradition of soldiering. We have no family anecdotes of wars or bombs. No thinly disguised careers in obscure government departments in Baker Street.

'What did you do in the war Daddy?' I had tried when I was a boy. 'Milkman,' he had said. The nearest I had got to the Great War was by our Uncle Jess. He was not really our uncle, at least I don't think so. He lived at the back of the shop in a filthy hovel which was unkempt, unordered, uncared for and absolutely chock-a-block full of treasure. His medals hung in a dirty picture frame on the yellowing wall. By the black iron fireplace stood an umbrella rack, home to all sorts of walking canes.

One day, I remember a funny gleam came into his eye and he said to me, 'Ere boy, git me that cane. The silver 'andled one.'

I inspected the silver handle in awe as I carried the stick back to him. It was fashioned into a horse's head but I was more impressed by the thought that this was silver. Real silver.

'You've nivver seen a cane like this boy. Eh?'

I shook my head. He grasped the cane in one horny, shaking hand and to my amazement, with a quick flick, he drew out a three foot long shiny steel blade.

'Swordstick! Go through you like a skewer that will.'

The end was wavering level with my stomach. His bony hand was shaking. It had been shaking since nineteen sixteen. I began to go red in the face from holding my breath.

'Frightened yer, eh boy?'

I nodded. My admission pleased him. I had to help him

resheath the blade which I did with great care for it was honed to a razor's edge. That was Uncle Jess who had gone to war as a lad and come home as an old man.

The lines of white gravestones basked mutely in the sun. Jess had come home. These had not. I could see the lines of stones as lines of soldiers sitting back to back. Real men, chatting, smoking, joking, drinking from their cans, waiting in this peaceful French countryside and wondering. I could not picture them dying however hard I tried. I could see them doing all the other things but not dying, so why had they? Why hadn't they come home like Jess? This cemetery posed me so many questions. So many questions and yet they were all one: why?

I sat quietly for a time, just thinking. The way I saw it, wars were not started by soldiers. Uncle Jess had not known any Germans; why would he have wanted to kill any? Wars were started by politicians and generals. I couldn't see any of their graves here. If it hadn't have been for them, these people might still have been living. The lines of soldiers all stopped what they were doing and turned their scornful eyes upon me. Had I only just realised THAT? They were wasting their time with me. As I watched, they slowly melted back into stone.

A Commonwealth War Grave on a quiet summer's day ought to be a compulsory meeting point for potential adversaries. This would test their mettle. I would defy them to rant and rave at each other, to threaten and posture in the name of peace, before the bitter silence of those upon whom an early peace had been forced against their will.

I sat down with my pen and pad at the roadside, carefully choosing my position to give me the prospect that I desired. Sketching in the arches, inking in the shadows and shading in the bricks allowed me to work away some of the confusion and profundity in which I had ensnared myself. I had to concentrate on the basic form of the monument, not its meaning. I was forced to consider its place on the page and not its place in history.

A large silver BMW, British registered, roared off the main road and onto the track leading to the cemetery. It stopped before me in a cloud of rattling pebbles and swirling dust, completely blocking my view. The driver's door swung open and, easing his paunch from under the steering wheel, a man wriggled out. He left the door open and the engine running and swaggered across to the archway, pulling up the seat of his trousers and trying to tuck into the waistband a shirt that was concertina'd from too many hours sweating in a car.

In the front passenger seat an owlish pair of enormous sunglasses flicked listlessly the pages of the Sunday colour supplement of an English newspaper. Obviously as far as they were concerned, I did not exist. To park directly in front of a person who was clearly sketching when there was available, a hundred yards of track, could not have been done on purpose. Nobody was that callous. I was there twenty minutes, during that time the engine was running and the pages were flicking over. Eventually I continued my journey, leaving the sketch to be finished later.

I still wonder whether the soldiers talked to baggy pants and whether he listened.

I rolled into Arras on a wide boulevard which encircled the town. A road like this could only mean one thing in France. The town must have been a fortified walled city and the walls had been demolished to make the road. It always happened that way.

In Paris, for example, they had done it twice. The city's fortifications had been razed in the eighteenth century to form the *Grands Boulevards* – the *Boulevard St. Martin, Boulevard Bonne Nouvelle* and so forth. Then they built another circle of walls around the growing city. These, they dismantled in the nineteenth century to form the *Boulevards Extérieurs.* You see, the problem with walls around a town is that they cause immense traffic jams as you can only leave or enter through a gate.

After the second lot of walls around Paris, events got a little out of hand and they began to build another circular road – the famous *Boulevard Périphérique* – without first erecting a wall to demolish. In fact, now that I think of it, the French word *boulevard* comes from the verb *bouleverser,* meaning, 'to upset' – which was what they did to the city walls to make the roads. I wouldn't quote me on that. I don't know where I learned it from. Probably from the same guide book that tells you about the galloping horses at the Mont St. Michel.

I intended to eat properly tonight. Agreed, that had been my intention on the previous nights but tonight I would concentrate on that one task and subjugate all others to it. I chose a commercial hotel in the centre of Arras, near the station. I strode into the hallway and made for the sign, *réception,* wondering what kind I could expect.

'Does your restaurant open this evening madame?'

'But, certainly, sir. Seven o'clock.'

'May I have a room with a shower please?'

'You may.'

'Is there somewhere I may put my bicycle?'

'Yes, the hotel has an underground car park. The entrance is down the street at the side. If you cycle around there I will open the door for you.'

Simple when you know how.

I showered, I ate, I slept. I awoke as a new man ready for what the day could offer me. At breakfast, I spread the jam on my tartine and the map on the table. I mention this mundane achievement because I took it as confirmation that I had finally exorcised the Curse of France. Well, we can all be mistaken.

I crammed my mouth full of fresh bread rolls, unsalted butter and jam and washed the plug down my throat with coffee which tasted like coffee rather than an insipid approximation. I would make today a challenge day. Arras and Amiens were only fifty miles apart. A perfectly decent main road ran between them so I would endeavour to travel from one to the other without going on it. I perused the map. Perhaps I would allow myself a maximum of one mile on the main road. One mile in fifty. Two per cent.

The sun was breaking through the cloud as I checked my milometer at the bus stop outside Arras railway station. At half past nine I pushed off southwards, over the railway bridge and turned into a road through an industrial estate. This left me with approximately seven eighths of a mile of main road in my allowance and fifty miles of journey to complete.

A little after midday I trundled gently into one of those straggling villages whose existence seems to hang on a thread. It was deserted, because it was lunchtime. Farms lined both sides of the main street. Parked outside them, tractors and dusty Peugeot pick-up trucks slowly ticked in the sun. Not a soul stirred. Not even a cat, as the French say. This is one of the most rewarding times to cycle because between the magic hours of twelve noon and two in the afternoon you can be certain that every Frenchman who has ever soiled a napkin will be firmly wedged behind a *plat du jour* and a bottle of *vin rouge*. You will have the road to yourself.

It is an astonishing truism that you may drive through such a village at such a time, in a square wheeled Simca with a lace-rusted exhaust pipe silencer, towing an iron waggon laden with empty cans and angular stones and you will disturb nobody. No shutters will angrily fly open to protesting shouts of *'Oh là!'* No little boys will whistle through their fingers at you. However, should you dare to freewheel through such a village on a silent running, well oiled, expertly maintained bicycle you will arouse from their slumbers all the demon dogs of hell.

The first was a mastiff-based mongrel with a head like a pot scourer. He was safely enclosed in a front garden by a five foot high chain link fence at which he launched himself and with a passionate conviction, conveyed his intentions should he find a hole in the aforementioned palisade. Next to him ran a low wall bordered by dinky conifer trees. This garden was apparently owned by a furry marrow which yapped and snapped at me as I appeared in each interstice. The relay was reluctantly adopted by a soporific alsatian which contented itself with lobbing a few 'woofs' at me from a sedentary position. And so on. By the time that I had reached the square in the middle, the formerly sleepy village had been brutally wrenched into dyspeptic consciousness by the uncouth observations of its dog population as it sonorously charted the progress of my incursion.

Under the drowsy shade of a plane tree, on a rustic bench sat two wizened men with faces like walnuts. One had a pipe, the other, a stick. They looked for all the world as if they were awaiting the arrival of their third member in order to adopt the pose of the three monkeys.

I ran my bicycle to the brown edge of the balding grass. Their eyes followed me accusingly for the uproar in the eastern half of the village had not yet subsided. Staccato yelping echoed harshly from the crumbling red brick walls of broken down barns, hollow barking rumbled through their sagging roof-timbers.

Near to the bench was installed a rubbish bin. Doubly incongruous in a country not renowned for rubbish bins, this one was, in its own way, magnificent. It lounged insolently on a concrete plinth rather as if it had deposed the war memorial. It stood about four feet six inches high and it was sculpted in canary yellow glass fibre. I gazed at it with the disappointment of a child who had been promised a bicycle and been presented with a hoop. France was the country which could entangle the entrances and exits of its underground railway stations in fantasy jungles of contorted green iron and yet France had erected this saffron suppuration.

It must have been the continued barracking of the disturbed dogs which goaded my brain into a short but ultimately repercussive period of activity because an unworthily diplomatic thought occurred to me. During the morning I had been unable to find a propitious place in which to discard my rubbish from the previous day. This rubbish consisted in the main of some small remains of my victuals, an empty sardine can and a split plastic water bottle. Surely, were I to leave an offering on the altar of garbage then I would be forgiven my flagrant incitement of the dogs?

Under the steady scrutiny of the monkeys' eyes I pulled the polythene bag from my pannier. You have to pack everything in polythene when you are cycling, there is no such animal as a waterproof cycle bag. With studied nonchalance I tossed the unwanted bag into the rubbish bin, remarking to myself that from the thud that it had made, I could deduce that the bin was empty.

This deduction led me to the proposition that perhaps the rubbish bin was brand new. Perhaps mine was the first rubbish. Perhaps it had not yet been commissioned and was awaiting the mayoral entourage to speechify, crack a bottle of champagne against its sides and cut the tape. And as the tape shrivels to the ground the applause staggers to a halt when the assembly realises that there is already a bag of rubbish in the bin. Oh the scandal!

I was still indulging my imagination with pictures of revolt and insurrection as I cycled out of the town which probably explains why I was so startled when a steel garden gate in front of which I was innocently pedalling, suddenly resounded with an explosion. It was the kind of crashing that you could palpably expect the gate to make were a ton and a half of freshly wrenched sugar beet to be inadvertently tipped against it. The subsequent blood-curdling yowl which ululated from the other side, however, gave lie to the leguminous hypothesis and indicated not only to me but to the entire village that there was a certain canine involvement.

Spurred on by the extra adrenaline that one's body deals out in times such as these in the interests of unashamed self-preservation, I rocketed past the garden and was half way along the next fence before an uncut dun coloured poodle, the size of a medium Jersey cow, noticed my flight and added his voice to the insults and oaths that were still being expectorated next door. This in turn alerted a ferocious but sly fox terrier. It crept up to its minute boundary wall in silence and then leapt up onto the top and paced me along the wall, yapping and spitting anti-British sentiments as it scooted up and down the castellations like a Roman centurion riding a monocycle along Hadrian's Wall.

The farms gave way to the gardens and the gardens petered out into that nondescript wasteland which lines the roads outside these villages like a parade of begging orphans. But still the *bourg* itself was in uproar. It was like VE day at Battersea Dogs' Home. I grinned with a mixture of mischief and relief. Well, they could bark as much as they liked now, I was out of it!

Pushing my best pedal downward I chuckled quietly as I recalled the sight of the two wizened monkeys watching me discard my rubbish. It was probably the highlight of their day. They would talk about it for weeks.

'Do you remember...?' one would say to the other. 'That beshorted apparition on a bicycle bedecked with bags, who woke up all the dogs just to throw his rubbish in our bin?'

'Ah yes,' the other would concur, 'and what a thud it made when it hit the bottom of the bin. Yes indeed.'

I chuckled again. What a thud! The dull mufflement of the impact was music to my ears. Yes. What a thud. Suddenly I braked so hard that both wheels skidded on the gravel. What a thud.

I had discarded a polythene bag containing an empty plastic water bottle and an aluminium sardine can and it had made a thud. Not a tinkle, not a clink, not a rattle but a thud. Try as I might I could not imagine a circumstance in which such musical instruments of fortune when hurled into a glass fibre bin would produce a symphony of 'thud'.

With a reluctance touching upon dread, I opened my front right hand pannier from which I had taken the rubbish and in which I habitually carried it. The top polythene bag contained a split plastic water bottle and an empty sardine can. I had not thrown away my rubbish, I had thrown away my pyjamas.

I wheeled my steed around and reluctantly pedalled back into the village which by now, had just sunk back into its rustic somnolence. I managed to swoop silently past the terrier but the Jersey poodle woke him and, rather unkindly, I thought, he added his protestations to those of the terrier despite his not having noticed me. Poor sportsmanship I call that. The terrier bobbed along the wall, the ton and a half of sugar beet emptied itself against the steel gate. I whistled nonchalantly into the square. On the bench the triumvirate was still missing one third of a quorum.

Until that moment I had never bothered to ponder the purpose of a rubbish bin but now, faced with the problem of getting something out of it, I realised how conceited had been my life to date.

Had I been struck in the face by a tepid flounder I could not have been more astonished than at that moment when I realised that rubbish bins were designed to be receptacles of rubbish; positively to welcome it, to throw open their doors and offer cream teas to it and to that end they were constructed to facilitate the ingress of the aforementioned detritus.

I invite you to picture the dilemma. The bin stood on a plinth, the plinth was surrounded by steps. I was immediately at a disadvantage of height by having to stand down on the top step since the plinth could not accommodate both me and its rightful incumbent. The flange surrounding the top of the bin distanced me further from my goal. I peered into it. It was empty, except for my pyjamas. I stretched my arm recklessly into the bilious maw. I could not reach the bottom. I squirmed, I twisted. The lip dug painfully into my armpit, my finger tips tantalisingly brushed the top of the polythene bag. I straightened up to regain my breath and met the stony stares of the two old men, the one with the pipe was frozen with his mouth open, the one with the stick was frowning.

There was nothing that I really felt like expressing at that juncture. Perhaps it was churlish of me but that was the way things were. I peered again into the jaundiced vase and noted morosely its similarity to the Venus Fly Trap. Except for the colour, of course. And my pyjamas.

I decided that such a desperate situation required a desperate solution, so rashly and without any regard for the continued artistic integrity of the receptacle, I hauled myself up onto the edge. It splayed and buckled. I plunged headlong into the bin, noting subconsciously before sinking below the horizon that I had seen daylight showing under the old men's bottoms. As I re-emerged, my pyjamas clutched in grim triumph and a polythene bag, the men were suddenly there at the side of me as if they had intended despatching me, in the style of Sweeney Todd. Before either could invoke some obscure infraction of the Cantonal law relating to the violation of rubbish bins, I announced, 'Pyjamas!' and opened the bag for inspection.

They peered in.

'Pyjamas,' Pipe said to Stick.

I hauled out the rightful bag from my pannier and flipped it open for a similar examination.

'Rubbish,' I declared.

'Rubbish,' Stick said to Pipe and flinched as I flicked it past him into the bin.

I left them standing there; two gnarled old men, gazing at the rubbish bin as if they had only just discovered its purpose.

The dogs?

Well they thought it was Christmas. They were still barking when I was a kilometre away.

chapter four

I can remember that my first French grammar book sported a map of Metropolitan France inside its front cover. Generations of my predecessors had updated and amended the cartography by drawing cartoon frogs riding bicycles and aeroplanes spiralling earthwards trailing plumes of smoke. I, being a mediocre artist and a fainthearted student left not a mark upon the battered text whilst it sojourned in my care but I did gaze often at the map, usually when I was supposed to be doing something else.

The result was that I made a sniggering discovery which, assisted by a hopelessly flawed process of assumption, laid the foundations for my admiration of French topographical nomenclature. The discovery was simply this. At the tip of the bit of the coastline which stuck out into the sea there was a town called Brest.

Now you will say that this observation is based on a complete misunderstanding of the language and is in no way justified but from that day onwards I began to believe that the French had a predilection for appropriate topographical names. Once an eleven year old boy knew that the Brest was the bit that stuck out it was very difficult to shake that belief. And as I got older I could still see some truth in it. What other country would dare to call a range of mountains by the definitive name of *Massif Central*? It has a Gallic pomposity about it with just a garlic-like whiff of insolence. *Massif Central.* No chance of ambiguity. You know exactly what they are and where they are.

There were two other French names to which I took a fancy. I used to think of them as a sedate married couple. Albert and Nancy. I had forgotten about them for years and now, I saw one signpost at a crossroads and the map was there before me in all its ink smeared, dog eared glory.

Albert.

I went wrong in Albert. I used some of my precious main road yards trying to find the supermarket. It was a cheat really because the main road did not look at all like a main road. It was a ribbon of tarmac laid over pavé and hemmed in on both side by lines of red-brick terraced houses. I bought some more bread, sardines and chocolate and a couple of rosy apples which caught my eye but later turned out to be floury. It was my own fault. I usually avoid red apples for just that reason.

As soon as I had left the supermarket I turned down a side road. I had calculated that there remained available to me about a quarter of a mile of my main road allowance. I was still thirty kilometres from Amiens as the crow flies but I knew where I was going. I would cycle direct south to pick up the valley of the Somme and then run along the small road alongside the river. Looking at my map, a name caught my eye. Cérisy. Where had I seen that name before? Cérisy. 'Water rumpling at the stern...' It was a poem wasn't it? *'Hospital Barge at Cérisy'.* One of the First World War poets. Graves or Owen or somebody. It was a text that I had done at school. I had to go there.

I chirruped through villages whose names meant nothing to me but which would stir in my memory years later when I read Siegfried Sassoon. I crossed the flat marshy valley of the Somme, bridging the canal near an estaminet called *Rendezvous des Pecheurs* or some such thing. I began to believe that the Somme was a mythical river. Its steep-sided valley is a hotchpotch of irregularly shaped ponds retained by crotchety dams and sluices; of interesting tracks that lead enticingly away through luscious grass under the light green airy shade of the poplar trees only to fade out after a few hundred yards. And there is the canal. But I could find no river in the valley of the Somme.

In the village street an alsatian was panting as it watched a young lady painting. She was painting the fire hydrant. She was painting it a brilliant red, covering the faded carmine with sensuous strokes of crimson. I watched her for a while. Because I derived childish satisfaction from seeing the blob of grey-pink becoming smaller and smaller. Because of the magical mesmerising sequence of dip, tap, dab, stroke; but mainly because she had a jolly nice figure and had taken off her summer dress in the scorching heat. The wrap lay brazenly discarded on the grass verge some distance away as she painted on in her underclothes.

'*S'il vous plait mademoiselle?*' She turned at my voice and shaded her eyes with her brush hand. '*Le canal?*'

'You need to go down towards the camp site.' She casually pointed the brush down the road. I followed the gory bristles.

I did not know it at the time but this young lady was to give me some smug entertainment several weeks later at work. Purely by chance, I encountered a man whom I had never met before but who came from Cérisy. His provenance was not relevant to our short exchange of words but as he was leaving I mischievously threw in the remark, 'I see that at last you have had your hydrants painted. They needed it.'

'Hydrants?'

'In your village. What's-her-name did it. The girl with

the alsatian.'

'Yes, yes.' His jaw dropped open. 'That's Marie-France.'

'Well cheerio! I must go.'

'But...' His mouth was still open as I shut the door. I sometimes think that I am not very fair to people.

I found the Canal de la Somme to be a secretive waterway, brooding between dark banks, overgrown with trees and bulging bushes. I propped up my bicycle on a searing hot girder bridge and sat and peered into the waiting water. There was no hospital barge here. There was no barge at all. I felt myself becoming maudlin with the oppressive importance of so simple a place, so I pulled out my sketch pad and started to draw.

This was the life! A pen, a pad and a bicycle! No cares or anxieties to furrow my brow. The dogs were behind me, my pyjamas were in my panniers and from here on, the road to Amiens would be downhill all the way. Nothing more could go wrong now, could it? Could it?

I discovered to my chagrin that to the observation that there was no river in the valley of the Somme, I could add the qualification 'and no road either'. This was a bitter disappointment to me as I had looked forward to a level road sweeping me into Amiens but the road which I had identified on the map, in real life shunned the soggy valley and amused itself by lurching over the spurs which formed the valley wall. Up and down it went like a switchback. No straight levels; as soon as it had reached the summit of each spur it would plunge abruptly down the other side. It was quite tiring.

I paused at the bottom of one of these dips and studied the road ahead. Before me was a quarter of a mile of steady climb to a knoll of trees which marked the crossroads. A short distance up this yellow road I could see a car. It was stationary and something about its attitude worried me a little. I pedalled mechanically towards it in the beautifully balanced and measured movement which I had calculated would take me to the top but still keep me a reserve of strength and breath.

At the rear of the car a trim woman in high heels and a lightweight suit was frozen in the theatrical pose of somebody unexpectedly interrupted whilst pushing a car. The pressure she was applying to the back of the car had not even flexed her manicured finger nails. At my approach she stuck her bottom out a little more than the high heels made necessary and looked forlornly over her shoulder at me.

With a barely concealed sigh, I stopped. There are few things more annoying than having to interrupt a well-oiled pedalling cadence.

'Do you need any help?' I heard my voice enquiring.

'Oh that would be so kind.' She smiled dazzlingly and straightened up. The car did not budge one centimetre which confirmed my suspicion that it was secured by the handbrake. I laid my bicycle down onto the grass verge and looked sideways at the vehicle. It was one of those cars that was all mudguards and bug-eyed headlights and which could be encountered bouncing along the byways of France in great numbers. I, of course, had managed to find one that had lost its bounce.

'What is wrong with it?'

'It won't start.' And to confirm her diagnosis it cleared its throat.

'Chick aha aha aha heurrr.'

'Did it stall on the hill?'

'No, we couldn't get it to start.' I looked around in wide-eyed astonishment. There was no sign of habitation anywhere. You don't just try to start a car in the middle of nowhere. She caught my eye and had the good grace to look quickly away and blush. 'Anyway,' she offered in explanation, 'they always say if you have trouble you should try starting the car on a hill.'

I shot her a quick glance to see if she was poking fun but

from the frank manner in which she met my eyes and shrugged, I drew the conclusion that she really did believe that cars started better on hills just by their being there. I thought that it would probably cause her pain if I explained to her that the technique was to run the car down the hill using the momentum of the vehicle to turn over the engine and help it to start and that was why cars started better on hills, so I said nothing. The car was facing uphill. Unfortunately the road was not wide enough to enable the car to be turned, so I went to the back. I watched her as she pushed the silver bracelets up her wrists and gingerly applied the balls of her fingers to the rear of the car.

'Ready?' I called to her female driver.

'O.K.' She called back and I heaved at the bumper. The front of the car dipped towards the tarmac and it groaned without moving. I cursed quietly under my breath.

'Take the brake off!' I shouted.

The brake came off with a bang and we skittered madly backwards by three feet.

'Put the brake on!' I yelled frantically. The car stopped. I had pushed this type of car several times before, admittedly not uphill, but I had not remembered it being so heavy. I inspected it critically whilst my assistant trimmed a broken nail. The car was tilted down to one side. Surely they had not got a puncture as well? When I went to confer with the driver, however, all was explained. The interior of the car was crammed with the largest woman I have ever seen in my life. The steering wheel was impressed into her bosom like a favourite nephew and the gear lever jutted out from under her armpit like Long John Silver's crutch. I could not for the life of me see how she had got into the car in the first place. I came rapidly to the conclusion that she must have gone to the factory and had the vehicle assembled around her.

I introduced myself and invited her to attempt to start

the engine. She turned the key and whilst the engine lethargically rumbled, coughed and spluttered she effectively stamped upon any spark of life by pumping the accelerator pedal up and down as if she were inflating a Zeppelin with a foot pump. This technique ensured that the car would not start for at least another five minutes because she had now flooded the carburettor with petrol. I was presuming of course that these cars did have a carburettor; an uncharitable doubt perhaps but then they seemed to have very little of anything. I eventually agreed to work on the assumption that even the French could not do without a carburettor.

How could I convince this monumental woman that all our interests would be best served by her dismounting and walking alongside? I turned to my manicured companion.

'I wonder if I could ask you to take the wheel?'

She smiled sweetly.

'I regret, monsieur, I do not drive.'

'Out of the question!' The driver decreed gruffly. 'She is not insured. And in any case my doctor has forbidden me to push.'

I looked about me as insolently as I could for her doctor but we were still just three figures in a landscape. With the car as 'still life'. I retired hurt, consoling myself with the thought that I could not in any case see how to get her out of the car without unbolting it panel by panel. Perhaps by unrolling the canvas sun roof and hoisting her out with a crane....

'I am going to try to bump-start you,' I explained. 'When I shout, let in the clutch.'

'Understood,' she replied in a businesslike manner.

I took the strain of the weight of the car.

'Release the brake!'

I began the back breaking effort to overcome the car's desire to descend the hill backwards. Slowly it began to roll forwards up the hill accompanied by my little, powerful steps pattering on the road.

'O.K. Let the clutch in!' I shouted.

'Chick ger rer rer rer.' The starter whined. What was she doing?

'Put the brake on!'

We stopped. I took a few sharp breaths and then proceeded forrard.

'Don't try the starter, that won't do it,' I explained in a kindly tone. 'Put it in gear.' She fiddled with the umbrella handle under her right armpit. 'And push the clutch pedal down. When I shout, let in the clutch and the momentum of the car will turn the engine over. O.K.?'

'Understood.'

'Let the brake off!'

We were slower to start this time but gradually we wound up to a decent speed.

'Let the clutch in!'

She did, with a vengeance. She must have selected first gear. The car stopped dead and like a cartoon character, I spread-eagled myself across the back with my nose squashed flat on the rear window. Fortunately, my assistant had already been left behind so she was unhurt.

'Put the brake on!'

Rubbing my nose and trying to breathe deeply at the same time I addressed the driver with a certain amount of reserve. I was sure that she could detect in me a barely suppressed tension and I did not wish to upset her.

'Try putting it in third,' I suggested.

'Third?' She lunged the umbrella handle gearstick into the dashboard. 'Understood. Ready?'

I walked slowly to the back of the car and nodded at my assistant who was straightening the pleats in her skirt.

'Take the brake off!'

Nothing was going to stop me now. I was determined to start this car. My back cracked and the blood pounded in my temples as I used all my reserves of strength to propel this useless lump of metal up the hill. Faster and faster, I was going to make sure that this time we had enough momentum to overcome all problems. Vaguely I was aware of my assistant stopping to put her high-heeled shoe back on again but the withdrawal of her effort did not reduce our velocity. Push, push, faster, faster.

'Let in the clutch!'

The car began to buck in slow motion, first the back kicked up and then the front, then the back again. It was the bucking horse in the children's playground. We are slowing down and not a spark of life can I hear in the engine. It seems to be turning over like dead metal, It was almost as if... 'Oh no!' I thought, 'Not that!'

It was imperative that I speak to the driver. Still pushing hard, I crept around to the side of the car, shifting my grasp from the back to the side window. Like the Lone Ranger clambering along the side of a runaway Wells Fargo stage coach, I worked my way along the side of the car, hand over hand, pushing all the while. A final lunge and I made it to the driver's window. One glance at the dull dashboard was sufficient.

'Turn the ignition on!' I shouted.

'But you said–'

I took another deep breath. The muscles in my arm were burning, my feet were stinging.

'Just – turn – it – on,' I panted.

She hastily groped in the folds of her flowered dress down by her midriff and a splinter green light appeared on the dashboard.

'Kerfuta kerfuta kerfuta kerfuta tuddle tuddle uddle uddle.'

Magically, like a dove taking flight from my hand, the hated car slowly pulled away from me under its own power. I stopped and bent myself double trying to catch my breath, my shoulders heaving, spittle dribbling from my mouth and falling to the road, my hands shaking with the effort. The car turned at the crossroads, which were only about fifty yards away and then came bouncing gaily back down the hill.

'Merci monsieur!' she shouted as she lolloped past me. I had only the strength to raise a flaccid hand in salute and roll my eyes. Still gasping painfully, I watched her stop and pick up her companion who waved to me before mounting in the car. A toot on the horn and they disappeared down the road and around the corner. I hobbled uncertainly after them to where my bicycle was lying three hundred yards below me.

I sat on the saddle and allowed my eyes to travel slowly up the long, straight, steady, climb before me. To the little knoll of trees that I had noticed ten minutes earlier. I took a deep breath and wearily worked myself into the mechanical pedalling cadence that I had known would get me to the top with ample reserves of strength and breath.

By half past four I could see Amiens laid out below me like a map. I had been cycling along a network of forgotten minor roads which crisscrossed the extensive acres of potato cultivations on the hill top. The reason why I had stopped was not to gaze upon Amiens but rather to inspect a pipe which sprouted out of the corner of the field. It looked for all the world like a fire hydrant and it was the third or fourth that I had noticed. Leaving aside the prohibitive cost of installing a permanent fire-dousing system around a field, I could not imagine sixty acres of potato plants to be particularly vulnerable to either spontaneous combustion or arson.

I was able to resolve my perplexity a few minutes later when I came across two tractors blocking the road whilst their drivers chatted to each other.

'Excuse me. Could you tell me what is the purpose of the pipes that I have been seeing on the edges of the fields?'

'Irrigation. It's for watering the crops.'

'Where does the water come from? We're on top of a hill. It must have to be pumped up.'

The farmer jerked his head towards the bottom of the valley behind me.

'It comes from the factory down there.'

'What kind of factory?'

'Potato starch. They pump all the waste water up here and we grow potatoes with it.'

The two men looked at each other and then guffawed. I was not certain whether the joke was in what he had said or whether it was me. But he was right. Several years later I had cause to inspect a map depicting water pollution in this area and, sure enough, the potato starch factory was featured as a major contributor to river pollution. This irrigation system was presumably one way of reducing the amount of effluent discharged into the Somme. I was not certain that I liked the incestuous idea of watering potatoes with the waste products of their forefathers. I was worried that it might produce a strain of mutant spuds.

Eventually I had to interrupt their conversation again to ask if they could move their barricade of tractors. Did they believe that I had cycled all the way from England to climb this hill, ask them what the pipes were for and then turn around and retrace my steps?

I rode into Amiens by the back door. I crept in through the *hortillonages* which I can only describe as a sort of watery allotments. Most of the plots are completely surrounded by narrow canals of brackish water and only accessible by flat-bottomed boat. Here, the Amienois grow primeurs and fruits for the local markets as they have done since the Middle Ages. And I didn't copy that straight out of a guide book. I happen to know somebody who owns one of these *aires* as the individual gardens are called and he explained it all to me.

My carefully chosen route joined the main road about

one hundred yards north of the railway station outside which I stopped at five thirty. The workers of Amiens were beginning to hurry back to the suburbs and had no time for me. Busily, they disgorged from buses and cars and invested the railway station. I sat in the yellow afternoon sun and watched them. Arras to Amiens. Over fifty miles and less than one mile of it on main roads. I was smugly contented with what I had achieved and for once, pride did not come before a fall.

chapter five

After several nights lodging in hotels I developed a fluid proficiency in wheeling my encumbered bicycle into the most unlikely places for it to sleep. The ability to unerringly guide my machine down a narrow, unlit corridor whilst standing behind it with one hand on the saddle was to inspire the confidence of hotel proprietors who would otherwise have vacillated between telling me that I would have to chain it up outside the hotel and suggesting that I pay for a garage space.

When breakfast was finished in Amiens, I edged past the hat stand and went down the corridor to the back door which led to the covered yard where I had left my bicycle. I was not prepared for the sight which met my eyes. When, on the previous evening, I had guided it in the darkness into the yard I had incidentally remarked that we were scrunching across gravel. By the light of the morning I could see my error. It was not gravel, it was broken glass. Generation upon generation of bottles had been smashed in this yard. From wall to wall stretched a glittering carpet of broken glass of all hues. Not one square centimetre remained uncovered. As I surveyed my sparkling white habitat I felt like the miniature figure on top of a giant Christmas cake. Indeed, I had no way of knowing whether underneath it all the ground was marble or marzipan.

I gingerly extricated the machine and half carried it through the hotel reception to the front pavement. I made a mountain of my bags against the wall of the hotel and then set to work to clean the tyres. They looked like enormous iced *beignets*, frosted with powdered glass and decorated with odd slivers of green and brown, like candied peel. As I extricated each shard I held my breath, expecting to hear the dreaded hiss of escaping air. Nearly at the end of the exercise, the street sweeper opened the stopcock at the corner of the street, allowing a torrent of clear water to run down the gutter and I took immediate advantage of this boon and washed away any residue.

Several passers-by graced me with the kind of benevolent expression that they would use for harmless lunatics. After all, why should anybody want to wash the tyres of a bicycle? Luckily, I am not a sensitive person and can rise above such inferences.

Amiens is the Préfecture, or the 'county town', of the département of the Somme. It used to be famous for its cloth industry, especially its velvet but I found nobody who knew anything about it. They all wanted to talk about the short-lived Peace of Amiens which ensued after the despicable English had signed a treaty here with Napoleon in 1802 and which they had then broken in 1803. Apparently we English had not realised that Napoleon also controlled Belgium, the Netherlands and Spain and so when all these territories celebrated the lifting of the British blockade by slapping prohibitive import duties on British goods, we decided that recommencing the war would be more profitable than peace. Thus Napoleon assembled his invasion force in Boulogne and sat back and awaited his fleets from the Mediterranean and Spain to move north and escort the invasion barges to England.

A measure of how seriously we took the threat of Napoleon's invasion can be acquired by inspecting the vast defences on the south east coast of England. The Western Heights underground fortifications in the cliffs of Dover; the Martello Towers erected a cannon's throw one from the other in a line from Folkestone to Eastbourne and the Royal Military Canal zig-zagging its thirty seven miles around Romney Marsh were all intended to defeat the evil 'Boney'. As it turned out, of course, it was all a waste of effort. Whilst Napoleon waited at Boulogne for his escort ships, Nelson and his mates were busy sinking them off Cape Trafalgar.

Once, I came across a Frenchman standing in Trafalgar Square and gazing in a rigor mortis of disbelief at Nelson's Column.

'England is the only country I know where they celebrate so magnificently their defeat in battle,' he observed.

'But we won the Battle of Trafalgar,' said I.

He pointed at the guano encrusted figure aloft.

'Nelson didn't win. He was killed. What sort of victory do you call that?'

I turned a blind eye.

For me, Amiens will always mean the long wait in the Paris-Calais express whilst indefinable technical operations are carried out. A black writhing hose will suddenly snake over the carriage roof and thrash a jet of water onto the empty track alongside. Down the platform, a man in blue overalls will push a trolley transporting a brutally greasy spanner and a bunch of daffodils. An employee in railway uniform will pass along the empty compartments, pulling cardboard tags from the tops of the seats and wrenching the heating lever back. The entire train will express indecision, jolting first forwards then backwards. The passengers just want to get to Calais but nobody seems to be in a hurry to assist them for it is here, at Amiens, that the electrification system of the old Northern Railway Company gives up. The electric locomotive which has hauled the rake up from Paris has to be discarded and two diesel locomotives have to take its place. Whilst this manoeuvre is being carried out, sundry officials, vendors and wheeltappers materialise from offices with opaque glass windows and swarm over, under and about the stranded carriages.

Amiens was the turning point in my cycle journey, I had to reluctantly acknowledge that by the end of the day I would have turned towards home. This in no way reduced the adventure of it all but it slightly dampened the enthusiasm of the day. It was like cycling in a limbo. Now I knew how a piece of flotsam felt at dead water when the tide was neither flowing nor ebbing. I was aimless. Then I had a stroke of luck.

I had already resigned myself to the probability that all the roads leading out of Amiens in a northwesterly direction would be busy with a fairly heavy industrial traffic. I had decided that I would just have to make the best of a bad job and try to break out onto the quieter roads as soon as the opportunity presented itself. And suddenly it was there! I had not even left Amiens but was just crossing the canal (with still no sign of the river) when I saw the towpath. It was a magnificent alley of smooth tarmacadam, a vehicle width, stretching off around the curve. This was the obvious way out of Amiens.

I consulted my map and although the towpath was not shown on it, I could see that the canal ran a few miles up to a bridge where I could join a minor road.

Ignoring the two signs which stated categorically that no vehicles were allowed, I turned off down the path. All became quiet as I left the roar of the rush hour traffic quickly behind me, bowling along to the swishing of my tyres on tarmac. On my left was the broad *Canal de la Somme* and on my right was a line of gardens with the odd glimpse of a *pavillon* or house at the far end. After a few hundred yards the gardens finished and the tufts of grass which began to appear intermittently in the middle of the track, I knew from experience, were happy portents of a rarely used and thus, peaceful route.

Away to my right now stretched water meadows which yard by yard, nudged the main road further and further away from me. By now the track was just two lines of tar and I was not at all alarmed when the minute flints began to twang and ping from under my tyres. When I ran onto the stretch of brickbats and broken clay pipe I experienced a little discomfort from the bucking of the bicycle and twice I laughingly imagined that I had nearly swerved into the canal itself. This was subtly made more possible by the behaviour of the straggling, overgrown hedge which had nestled cosily up to the edge of the towpath, forcing me out towards the canal. As if in sympathetic understanding of the desires of the hedge and the canal to unite, the towpath contracted to a single rut of lumpy dried mud. It became worryingly obvious to me that I could only put my right foot down to steady myself since my left would go straight into the canal.

Then I came to the breach in the bank.

Actually, I am exaggerating to say that it was a breach. The bank had softened and crumbled away taking with it my muddy rut. For a distance of a few feet the canal water lapped at the roots of the hedge. I came to a slithering halt, remembering to fall to the right. I surveyed the obstacle whilst wishing fervently that the clump of nettles into which I had just thrust my bare right leg could have found somewhere else to flourish.

I don't give up easily but my first reaction was to call myself nine kinds of a fool for not having turned back earlier. I then considered the practicality of a rapid volte face but realised that I had ignominiously ridden into the trap. There was hardly enough room to dismount, let alone turn the bike around. I did not feel myself skilled enough to wheel the loaded bicycle backwards along that rut without overbalancing into the canal. This was a bit different from a hotel passageway. The truth was, I had to go on.

Without the bicycle I could jump the gap easily. I could almost step over it. I decided that the first thing to do in any case, was to lighten the bike. I dismounted heavily to my right throwing myself into the hedge to give myself enough room. The hedge, realising that I was playing a game, gently bounced me and my bike back towards the canal. I overbalanced and lurched head forwards. For a terrifying moment, I stared at the black water, toe-teetering at that point of no return that you all have experienced. Very slowly, I sank back onto my heels and my legs immediately began to shake with fright. I don't like water. I have always been scared of canals. And I cannot swim.

Gingerly, I began to unhitch the front pair of bags. This necessitated my leaning right over the front wheel towards the murky canal whilst holding the bike upright and trying to ignore the spiky pieces of hedge that were trying to insinuate themselves into the naturally prominent portion of my anatomy. I lifted the bags from the carrier. They were the type that were joined together by a flap. I held this and swung them gently back and forth in preparation for throwing them across the gap. If they fell short, they would disappear for ever, if I threw them too hard then they could still roll into the canal. I weighed them as they swung backwards and forwards. They had the aero-dynamics of a pair of Wellington boots. I wished that I had watched the men playing boules in Montreuil instead of posing with my sketchpad.

Arguing vociferously with each other, like wildcats with their tails tied together, the two bags hurtled over the water to land with a sickening squelch safely on the other side. Now to the back bags. These were separate and had to be detached individually. The elastic shock cord on the first bag came off with a twang which threw the bag upwards and sent the tenuous partnership of man and bike resonating alarmingly. I backed into the hedge which ushered me forwards again. I swung the bag like a pendulum. It was neat, it was compact, it would go a long way. I did not want it to. I tried to lob it up so that it would fall vertically and not roll and was amazed to see it describe a steep arc and land squarely on the patch of ground that I had targeted. Perhaps I was not such a duffer at sports after all. If only they had tried me out at school with hurling the cycle bags instead of giving me cannon balls and spears to throw, then I might have distinguished myself.

Flushed with success, I quickly detached the remaining bag and imitated the first lob. Unfortunately, in its graceful, measured, sweeping, upwards movement, the bag caught the end of my handlebars and catapulted off on a low trajectory. I was hastily occupied during the ensuing few seconds in trying to regain the balance that the blow to the handlebars had so badly jeopardised, but not too busy to notice the flight of the bag. It impacted on the very edge of the breach and then took to the air like a Barnes Wallis bouncing bomb. It leaped over the other bags and bounded out of sight into the long grass. I listened for a splash but realised, morosely, that it would probably slide quietly into the water, sink to the bottom and then explode when it reached twenty fathoms.

Now the bicycle. I briskly slipped my left arm under the crossbar and hoisted the lightened bike onto my shoulder like an overcoat. Without giving myself time to worry too much I simply grabbed a bundle of hedge and swung myself and the bike around the pivot of my right arm and leg. I could hardly believe my good fortune when I made neat and precise contact on the continuation of the path. It was with a quiet jubilation that I strapped the muddy and bruised bags back onto the bike. I discovered even that the lost bag was only cowering in the long grass. My fears were unfounded though. The canal obviously considered that it had put me to the test and I had passed with flying colours and pannier bags and so it abruptly veered away from the towpath and kept a six feet margin of bulrushes between us. The towpath, however, took umbrage at this and just stopped. Before me was a solid wall of foliage and grass. Nobody had been along here this year. Convinced that there existed a semblance of a path under the paraphernalia of nature, I simply rode at it, tearing through the branches and bounding over the tufts of grass which were hidden below the nettles.

At this point I would like to take you further along to the bridge which was to be the goal of my shortcut. Here, a well-used but minor road crosses the *Canal de la Somme* on a solid concrete bridge. Under it, the towpath has been gritted and the fishermen often park their cars there. The fifty yards of the towpath adjacent to the bridge have been cleared back for a distance to provide a terrace and car park for a pretty little estaminet. The brightly painted wooden shutters and the highly coloured floral baskets of this bistrot can be seen from the road long before the crossing is reached and so the traveller is amply informed of its presence which he acknowledges by stopping and refreshing himself in large numbers. In short, the café is very popular. The tables outside are largely occupied by discreet couples, gazing dreamily into each others' faces whilst the shady interior houses the boisterous lorry drivers and travelling reps.

I have taken the liberty of introducing the scenario

thus, to permit you, the reader, to live and relive the astonishment experienced by these people on that placid summer morning. As they sipped their pastis and made small talk, suddenly, from the far end of the car park, a cycle burst through the impenetrable mass of interlocked foliage, showering leaves and twigs onto the nearest table. A woman shrieked, a chair fell over, men started forwards and then stopped. The bicycle continued on its course, dragging a small branch with it and chopping up and spitting out little bits of leaves. The garish red bags were spattered with mud, and blood was running along the top of the rider's thigh where he had been sliced by a bramble.

'Good morning everybody. Please don't get up. Lovely day isn't it?' I said in English as I rattled across the car park and up onto the bridge.

When I was quite clear, I stopped and removed the greater part of my camouflage but one bundle of grass I left jammed in between the front carrier and the wheel hub. It stayed there for the rest of the journey, for the rest of the summer. It went brown, it went white. When anybody asked me about it I would say, 'I got that at the Somme.' It eventually dried up and dropped off my wheel in November but I didn't see it go.

I had intended to phone home at some time during the day and having pinpointed where I would have lunch, I was making my way towards the town with the strength of stroke that anticipation of a solid meal gave me, when I saw the telephone kiosk.

In a former working life, I had used public telephones extensively in France. I had frantically scribbled down barely heard orders from a polished aluminium phone beneath the booming tannoy of Orly airport; I had pompously 'taken a communication' in the numbered wooden kiosks which squatted in the yellow basement of the all-night post office in the Rue du Quatre Septembre; I had phoned, squashed between a juke box and a sandwich toaster; I had paddled about in the cellars of bars where the taps never stopped dripping and customers kept mistaking the cubicle for the toilet. I had even, and this is no word of a lie, regularly used the very same Parisian café telephone that was shown in one of the sequences of the film of *The Day of the Jackal*.

But all this was in a previous existence. I had been away. The equipment had evolved, the coinage had changed. Like many gradual changes, when espied from across the river, the whole waterfront had changed.

So when I first saw this telephone kiosk, sitting boldly erect on the little green bank, I did not initially recognise it. An island of aluminium and glass in the midst of earth, grass and stone. It was only when I pondered which road to take at the fork that I realised what it was.

Along with the recognition of its outline came the appreciation of its function and its relevance to my situation. I could use this very kiosk to make one of my five franc calls to home. I had calculated that five francs furnished just sufficient time for both parties to exchange the essential news and instructions without admitting any leeway for irrelevancies. This kiosk's suitability was further enhanced from my standpoint by the provision of a soft bank against which I could lean my bicycle, the latter being unable to remain upright unaided.

Obtaining entry was not as straightforward as I would have desired. The first difficulty with these glass and metal kiosks is to identify the actual intended access. Each side of the cuboid monolith appears identical to its neighbour. One, I ruled out *ab initio* by the fact that it supported the telephone apparatus and I felt that it would be uncharitable in the extreme to infer that the French would extend their *architecture moderne* to the bolting of telephone apparatus to the door of the kiosk. Attacking the remaining three sides with the palm of the hand revealed a certain flexibility of assembly which manifested itself in a curiously bland rattle. To discover which panel served as the door I had to use a process of comparison and elimination of the rattles. This was necessary since nobody had apparently found a process by which this particular panel could be labelled, in a clear script at human eye level with, for the sake of argument, the word, 'door'.

Having found the door I was then confronted by the dilemma of whether to push or pull and, once decided, which side of the door to apply the pressure to. I worked the permutations. I pushed at the right side, it gave a little. I pushed at the left side, it did likewise. I pulled at the right side, it gave a little. I pulled at the left, it gave less. The result of my experiment seemed to suggest that the door lifted out entirely like a manhole cover – not a possibility that I felt I could really entertain. It was not a roller blind; it didn't slide up into the roof, nor did it lower to the ground like a drawbridge.

I turned my back on it, walked a few steps away and turned to regard it anew, just in case there was a patent factor that I had somehow overlooked. Such as a six foot high flashing neon arrow pointing to a servo control panel marked *'press here to open the door,'* but there was not.

What I did notice, however, was a fixing at the top and bottom of the door leading into the framework of the kiosk but not situated one end or the other as one would have expected of the classical hinge. The attachments were roughly two thirds of the distance along the door. At that position I knew they could only possibly be pivots. Warming to this, I quickly concluded that if this were so, then one portion of the door had to move inwards whilst the other swung outwards.

Tingling with anticipation I stepped up to the box and pulled the door with one hand whilst pushing the opposite end with the other. The cabin door swung open as if yawning with the boredom of my attempts to shift it. It was very easy and although a little stiff, probably due to its very occasional use, it was quite a neat arrangement. For the pleasure of the discovery and not for the insulation that it provided from the outside world, I swung it closed behind me. It really was quite simple.

I made my phone call with little difficulty. The tones sounded different and the hardware felt strange but the instructions were of the child's picture book type so I had no problem understanding them. This telephone kiosk was on a grass bank. It was somewhere vaguely near three isolated houses on the minor road which ran along the side of the Somme valley that nobody used. I could not imagine why anybody should want to phone from here and yet whilst I was talking, a van pulled up. I could see its roof from the kiosk and the driver was obviously waiting to use the phone. My phone!

By the end of my call I was more than happy to relinquish my position, indeed I was curious to see who else could possibly require its facilities. The kiosk, however, had other ideas. It would not let me out. Whether I lost my powers of reason in panic or whether I had just paid insufficient attention to the operation of the mechanism, I could not tell, but the result was that I became confused and could not remember which portion of the door to pull and which to push. I rattled, I banged, I heaved, I cajoled, I swore; still I remained interned. In my confusion, had I overlooked a simple lever or catch that was preventing me from continuing on my way? I could find none.

I thought drastically of pocketing my pride and phoning the exchange for assistance, but of course the remainder of my money was on my bicycle, snugly reposing against that confounded bank that I had so admired.

I looked to the van for my salvation. I banged and shouted to attract attention but the driver had left his van's engine running and he could not hear me. I gave one bicep-tearing tug at the door and with a screech, one end opened approximately one inch. Madly, I clutched it with my finger tips and dragged it wider, two inches, four inches. I swivelled around and without releasing my grip, I pushed my knee into the other end. Six inches, then it stopped. I tried to squeeze myself out but desisted. If I had to choose, then I would prefer to be trapped inside the kiosk rather than jammed half in and half out.

In a frenzy of frustration, I braced my back against the telephone case and kicked my heel twice against the door. The gap opened to ten inches. With both hands I dragged the door, screeching and squealing, grinding and groaning into the open position. With as much gravity as I could muster, I stepped out, like Dr. Who from the Tardis.

'You took your time,' the man from the van said as he strode up to the bank.

'Well I...' I was flabbergasted.

'Some of us have to work you know.' He tapped his sheath of papers which were pinned to his clipboard, 'I've got a repair docket for that phone.'

'Well you're wasting your time.' My laugh was ironical. 'The phone works perfectly. I have just phoned England on it.' I expected him to be just a little impressed with that disclosure. There could not have been many people in this part of the Somme who had used that phone to make an international call.

'I don't care about the phone. I've got to repair the door. It sticks, apparently.'

I had heard of people claiming to be watched over by a guardian angel and I wondered if it were possible to ascribe a similar surveillance to a guardian devil.

And then I remembered the Curse of France.

chapter six

'Where has he gone then, Dédé ?'

'He's doing the schools.'

'With 4715 ?'

'No, he took the Tank.'

'They hadn't fixed the track rod end on it.'

The other coach driver shrugged non committally.

'He's not going far. Alex can fix it when he gets back.'

'You know the chief wants another driver for Canterbury tomorrow?'

'Well I'm out. Last time I went I put the cart through a cheese grater.'

'I remember.'

'So does the chief. Perhaps he'll send Aristide.'

They both laughed in an unkindly fashion.

'Why not?' One of the other drivers butted in, sucking the beer froth from his ginger moustache. 'They could always put him on a leash so that he doesn't get lost.'

I had fallen across this bar at lunchtime. The road had

led me to it through a depressing admixture of decaying agriculture and moribund industry. I had espied the dining tables through the side window and immediately scooted my bike into the shade of the corner porchway. And now I was leaning against the bar, eavesdropping on the conversations of the drivers from the coach garage across the square.

It was probable that this 'Aristide' they were talking about was short-sighted. Suddenly one of the men said, 'Look out, here he comes.'

Into the bar walked a little man wearing a neat blue overall and pebble glasses.

'Hey Risti! I heard the chief say that he was sending you to Canterbury tomorrow. Joel is sick.'

Aristide looked up at the band of grinning drivers and blinked at them.

'He says he's going to fit a radar on the 5910.'

'And tie a white stick to the front bumper!'

Aristide acknowledged their presence with a sad smile and then addressed the patronne with a polite, '*Un kir s'il vous plaît madame.*'

'*Oui monsieur.*'

'Go on Choux-Choux! Give him a kir in a braille glass!' The other drivers laughed derisively.

'*Merci madame.*' He took the glass and half turned away from the drivers to me. '*Santé monsieur!*'

I raised my glass to him and returned the salute.

Like a player in a village hall pantomime, the patronne walked out through the archway at the back of the bar and then in through the doorway further down the room, having attired herself in a white apron whilst backstage.

'Half past twelve! Lunch is ready!' she said.

We all walked through into the back room, leaving the bar deserted. The tables were waiting, each place already set with a jug of wine and a plate of hors d'oeuvres. It was boiled egg mayonnaise. The drivers went directly to their habitual places and then to her obvious surprise and consternation, Madame La Patronne noticed that there was one extra diner. Me.

'Monsieur?' she asked.

'Can one have lunch?' I enquired, ignoring the unvoiced suggestion that this was a private lunch club.

She looked about the buzzing dining room in naive confusion. The tables were full.

'But yes, er... I will put you here.' She turned hurriedly to the little man in pebble glasses whose name I knew to be Aristide. 'This does not disturb you, Monsieur Richard ?'

The old man looked up like a startled sparrow.

'But not in the least, madame.' He unfolded his napkin. 'Wine?' he asked me as he picked up the pichet.

'No thank you. I don't drink wine.'

Madame La Patronne, hearing my refusal, bore down upon me like a galleon.

'Would monsieur like a beer?'

'No thank you. Could I have a glass of water please?'

'But a pichet of wine or a demi of beer is included in the price,' she protested.

'But I don't drink wine or beer so I shall be quite happy with a glass of water.'

She studied me for a second as if it had occurred to her that I was being awkward by design and then she magnanimously announced, 'I shall bring you a bottle.' She returned with a bottle of Evian mineral water. As all the diners had launched themselves enthusiastically into their egg mayonnaise, guffawing loudly and showering the table with the shrapnel of bread crust, I asked if I could see the menu. Again, she eyed me curiously, the suspicion in her mind obviously not dispelled.

'There is no menu. That's the entrée.' She nodded at the eggs. 'And the main course is duck with turnips.'

She disclosed this information with such authority that I did not dare argue. That was the meal. I was going to eat it.

Let's hear no more about this 'menu' business.

'Monsieur is on holiday?' my table companion enquired.

'Yes, just wandering around.'

'Are you at the campsite?'

'No I am cycling around. I stay in hotels when I can find them.' I briefly scanned the room. 'You all work at the bus garage across the road do you?'

He smiled thinly. 'They work. I potter about the garage for their amusement.'

I didn't really know how to express my displeasure at their disrespect, so I just said, 'Yes, they seem quite a noisy team.'

He smiled again.

'You have a diplomatic way of expressing yourself. I know what you mean. It's my own fault really that they tease me. Well not my fault,' he corrected himself, 'but more my lot. It serves me right.'

'I don't see why.'

'I don't need to work. I am sixty nine. I have retired. I just do it to amuse myself.'

'I don't see why they—'

'When I was their age I did exactly the same. Worse even. They only tease me; 'Little Risti'. When I was an apprentice, I used to talk disparagingly about a chap we called 'Loulou' – Louis Breguet. Now he was somebody. They have more right to tease me than I had to talk disrespectfully about Monsieur Breguet.' I looked at him, my mind whirring. Louis Breguet? Louis Breguet? I searched in my memory. The name was vaguely familiar. Who was he? 'You have heard of Louis Breguet?'

'I have heard of him but I must admit that I cannot think of the context.'

'He put Marcel Dassault where he is today,' he remarked with a little contempt.

Of course – the pioneers of aviation. Blériot, Breguet, Farman, Voisin – they were the grand marques of airplane before the Great War.

'Did you work for Louis Breguet?'

'Not directly. I worked at Hispano Suiza. Breguet used our engines in his planes.'

Hispano Suiza! Another one of the magnificent names from a golden era of motoring and flying.

'They used to make those enormous cars didn't they? Whatever happened to them?'

'Well I retired on their pension nearly ten years ago.'

'From...?'

'From Hispano Suiza.'

I was quite dumbfounded. I had assumed that the company had foundered and disappeared along with such names as Delage and Levassor.

'You mean that Hispano Suiza still exists?'

'Yes they make marine engines now. They don't make aero or automotive engines any more.'

Madame came and cleared away the remains of the first course and placed the main course between us.

'I've put it all in one dish. It saves room. You won't fight over it will you?'

It was so matter-of-fact that I could not argue. It made logistic sense to put both portions on one serving dish. The fact that we two were complete strangers merely dining together through force of circumstances was ignored, it was not even considered to be a factor in the calculation.

The duck with turnips was excellent. I can say no better. Thinking about the countryside that I had ridden through, I could understand that the dish was more logical than the customary duck with orange. You don't grow oranges in the valley of the Somme but ducks and turnips I had seen.

'What did you do for Hispano Suiza? Were you a mechanic for them also?'

He appeared puzzled and then looked at his overalls.

'Oh I am not a mechanic, I'm just an odd job man. I put these on to keep my clothes clean. No, I started off at

Bois-Colombes in the drawing office. I worked up through there and then I went to Villacoublay.

'When I look back on it now it's frightening how everything has advanced. In those days, if a plane had an accident the pilot got told off, not buried. Now they kill two hundred, three hundred, sometimes five hundred at a time. It makes me shudder. We had a factory at the side, well on, the aerodrome at Villacoublay so we saw the planes quite often. I'll tell you one that we saw.' He dipped his finger in his wine and drew a question mark on the paper table cloth. I looked at it. The pink translucent wiggle was obviously supposed to mean something to me. Eventually I was forced to ask,

'Which one was that?'

He tapped the table.

'*Point d'interrogation.* That was the name of the plane. "Question mark". It was the one that first flew from Paris to New York non-stop. We built the engines for it. That must have been in... now let me see. Bellonte and Costes did it about three years after Lindbergh had flown the other way. That was in '27 so it must have been in 1930.'

'Did you ever see Lindbergh?' That was someone I had heard of.

'Lindbergh? No I never saw Lindbergh. I saw Maurice Bellonte quite often. He used to pop in and look at the engines.'

'Was it a twin engine plane then?' I prompted him. 'You said, "engines".' I wanted this man to talk.

'In 1930? To cross the Atlantic? They could never have carried the fuel! No, it was single engined. It was a Breguet 19 GR with our Hispano Suiza engine. Terrific engine. A V12, water cooled. The insides of the cylinders were like mirrors they were so highly polished. Just like mirrors. It hardly used any oil at all. That's quite important if you are flying for two days non-stop.'

'How many horse power did it produce?'

'Six hundred in the *Bidon*. That was what they called the Breguet 19GR, the "petrol can" because the fuselage was full of petrol. You know, for flying long distances. But the crossing was made in a *Super Bidon*. That produced six hundred and fifty horse power. Of course that's nothing nowadays but it was enough to get to New York. You know, when they came back, they came back by boat of course, they put the plane on deck in crates, well, after they came back they flew down to Villacoublay and did a couple of swoops over the factory for us on their way to Le Bourget. We all ran out and watched them. It was a sort of way to say "thank you". That was the kind of person Bellonte was.'

'How many engines did you build for them then?'

'Four I think. We put one aside to be put in the plane, then we put one on a test plane and flew it everywhere to see how reliable it was. That way we could work out what would go wrong with the other engine. Then we made all the modifications to another engine that we ran on the bench for two days and nights which was how long we thought that it would take them to do the crossing. We stripped that one down and looked at it and then incorporated all the modifications in the final engine which we had put aside at the beginning and then we put that engine into the airframe.'

I mulled over what he had said. It was astonishing if it were true.

'Do you mean that the engine that went into the record breaking plane was brand new? Never been run?'

'It had been run a little, to make sure that it worked, but not run like the others. You see,' he admitted candidly, 'although it was a good engine, you kept it fresher by not using it.'

'Tart or ice cream?' Madame demanded.

Like a fool I said 'ice cream' and duly received a slug of tinted frozen chemicals whereas Monsieur Richard, late of Hispano Suiza, was served with a golden brown tart laid with slices of apple. It was my own fault. I had seen many apple trees in the Somme but I hadn't seen one iceberg. When would I learn?

I pedalled up a deserted hill, leaving the Somme far behind me. The sun was now relentless and my very English legs were turning from marble white to salmon pink before my very eyes.

Did you know that you can always distinguish a cyclist by his sun tan? This can be quite a frightening experience to persons of delicate constitution: the moment when they first encounter a cyclist walking towards them up the beach. The apparition before their eyes looks like nothing on earth. The body is not tanned a uniform brown but burned violently in some spots and bleached in others.

As you cycle along, the sun singes the tops of the thighs and the backs of the calves for, quite naturally, it is these portions which are alternately presented, face upwards to the sun. By the same measure, the front of the lower leg and the back of the thigh never sees the warm caress of the carcerogenic ultra violets and so remains alabaster white. The ankles owe their ghostliness to the dainty socks in which cyclists habitually encase them, driven by the forces of a tribal fetish. The face suffers in like form. The forehead, nose and upper lip positively iridesce with calories whereas the lower jaw and neck mooch about in the lower registers of dirty milk. I suppose, in retrospect, it is hardly surprising that dogs bark at me.

Auxi le Chateau is where I am making for. It nestles in the valley of the river Authie which, you may remember, is sandwiched between and parallel to, the valleys of the Canche, up which I had cycled almost to Arras, and the Somme, down which I had cycled from Amiens. At Auxi I will settle into a hotel, enjoy a shower and perhaps pop out in the evening and drop pebbles into the clear water from an old stone bridge. They must have an old stone bridge.

The valley of the Authie, hitherto unknown to me, was all that I could have desired. The road ran through shaded knots of trees and alongside small fields of unidentifiable vegetables. It was peaceful and restorative for, I had begun to realize, four days of cycling, rather than toning me up was beginning to wear me down.

Auxi le Chateau was a disappointment. I could find no suitable hotel. There was one hotel in the middle of the town but I could tell from the way that it frowned at me through its ivy that we just would not get on together. This was confirmed by the tariff board hanging in the window. The discovery was a blow to me. I had rashly allowed my imagination to run free in the adventure playground of my mind. I had been practically towelling the steaming shower essence from my sinuous body as I had pulled up on the gravel outside. In my opinion, nothing can usurp pea-gravel as the most effective and brutal debunker of day dreams.

The next revelation was even more unwelcome. No matter which way up I held the map, it was obvious that if I did not find a hotel before I reached the next town, I would be unlikely to find one there, for the next town was Hesdin. It was inescapable. It squatted like a spider on the cobweb of my holiday. I was so upset by this discovery that I forgot to look for the bridge from which to drop pebbles and I never caught a glimpse of the chateau for which Auxi was named.

It was seven o'clock by the time that I crept into Hesdin. On the way there my chain had come off as I had attacked a long hill. I had alighted and put it back on again and then pushed the bike up the hill instead of riding it. It was not a particularly steep hill but I had created a dangerous psychological precedent. I had admitted that some hills might be considered too steep to be ridden up. Was this an early sign of defeatism?

I wasted no time in Hesdin. I knew the hotel stock and did not wish to renew old acquaintances. I started down the luscious valley towards Montreuil, repeating to myself with each weary turn of the pedals that I had remembered seeing a hotel when I had passed this way to Hesdin. It was certain to be just around the corner. Several kilometres and many corners later I did find the hotel. It was boarded up. My gloom deepened. To add to my difficulties, since my passage earlier in the week, an attempt had been made to resurface the road. I say that it was only an attempt because it was obvious that the man with the gravel lorry had forgotten the recipe and could not recall how many tankers of tar you mixed with how many lorry loads of gravel. And so the road now consisted of a stream of hot sticky tar, lightly sprinkled with two ounces of gravel and left to bake all day on sun, regulo 6.

I tried to navigate my machine from one peninsula of gravel to the next archipelago and then down the isthmus, followed by some sticky island-hopping before reaching the fringes of a continent once again. The tar pulled at my tyres exactly as you would expect molten tar to do. I can describe it in no better way.

Then around the corner came hurtling a huge, silver grey Citroen, rattling, rumbling and roaring recklessly over the threadbare carpeting and before I could predict the consequences, it rocketed past me in a stinging cloud of flying tacky-tarred gravel. I felt, burgeoning within me, a retrospective sympathy for the dull grey house of my paternal grandmother which, as an uncomprehending boy, I had watched being pebbledashed. I now knew how it felt.

After painfully picking the cloying gravel from my scalp and delicately disentangling it from the hairs on my legs, I mustered my last reserves of courage and pedalled onwards. Perhaps the unprovoked assault perpetrated upon my person served to shake up my reasoning for I did an ostensibly idiotic thing. I turned off the minor road onto an even more minor road which I had noticed running parallel; ghosting my movement along the valley floor.

No sooner had I joined it than I found a hotel. A hotel! It was there. Its illuminated sign swung gently from the neat white facade with a bravura which refused to admit that it was actually on the minor tributary of a minor road in the middle of nowhere.

Here, I knew there would be a room. There would be dozens. It was one of those hotels whose original reason for existence, if indeed there had ever been one, was now so obscured that it remained a commercial anomaly, living from day to day.

A welcoming red glow and an unseasonal warmth radiated from the enormous log fire which crackled in the entrance as I walked towards the lady with the steel spectacles, standing at the reception desk. Dropping my bags in a businesslike manner, I announced, 'I would like a room with a shower please.' I had decided that no matter what the price, I would have a room with a shower. I did not actually expect her to kiss the ground at my feet in an elaborate kow-tow and offer me the best room in the hotel but I was a little taken aback by her gentle, measured response.

'Je regrette monsieur, nous sommes complets.'

Full? What FULL? My jaw dropped in astonishment. What on earth could they be full with? I shot a glance at the key board. This hotel had thirty rooms. Was she trying to tell me that it was completely full?

'All right then, a room without a shower will do.'

'I'm sorry monsieur, but we are full. We have been full all the week. It is the fishing competition.' As if in corroboration, a sudden burst of many voices in straggling laughter and jeers came from the room behind her. 'It is the same every year.'

She was very, very sorry and kindly recommended another hotel, four miles further along the road. She was not, I felt bitterly, as sorry as I was. Subconsciously I had let my body go. I had told it that we had stopped cycling for today and it had believed me. I now had to catch the muscles before they clocked out, put on their coats and went home.

I wobbled noticeably as I pulled away from the hotel but I had time to register that the car park which had been concealed from me by outbuildings, was brimmed with cars. Not that I had disbelieved her, you understand, but it would have been a difficult story to accept on the twin proofs of her word and the sound effects emanating from another room.

The poplar trees dawdled past me, even the stream appeared to be travelling faster than me. After four miles I reached a deserted station. Next to it was the hotel, equally deserted. It is at times such as these that one is tempted to fling the bicycle over a hedge, change one's name and hitch a lift in a lorry travelling southwards. I am certain that cycling is far more beneficial to my mental wellbeing than my physical.

I was approximately eight miles from Montreuil-sur-Mer. At my present speed, if I could maintain it, the journey would take me an hour. I felt that at the next opportunity, I should cross the valley floor and join the main road to Montreuil. It was not a difficult decision to take. Apart from sleeping under a hedge, this would be my last chance of getting a bed for the night.

My legs turned mechanically, round and round. The road slowly rolled beneath my wheels. I was in bottom gear now all the time. Each time I came to a downhill slope I freewheeled almost to a stop before wearily pushing at the pedals again. I had never been so tired.

Joining the main road was nearly an insurmountable problem and I expended an important portion of my diminishing reserves of strength just to cycle up the hill and not suffer the ignomiry of having to dismount and push, although this latter action would probably have conserved my energy. I can be stupidly vain when I want to.

I staggered around the corner and half collapsed and half fell with relief onto the pavement. The corner building was a small hotel. The patronne fussed about me. She insisted that my tired cycle should sleep indoors in the banqueting room and although it was well past dinner time, she found me a plate of cold meat. What the French call *une assiette anglaise* and I had a room, albeit without a shower.

Just before turning in for the night, as I clinked and clonked down the loose-tiled corridor on my way back from the toilet, the timed light switch plunged me into blackness. Not quite complete oblivion though. Through the gaps in the roof I could see the moon and by the silvery light of moonbeam pencils, I picked my route back to my room.

chapter seven

Breakfast was no great affair. I ate it at the bar, standing elbow to elbow with the passing deliverymen. I had slept as soon as my head had touched the pillow and this morning my body felt gloriously loose. Whichever way I bent, whichever muscle I moved, it ached.

The patronne had enquired conversationally where I had come from and when I had said, 'Amiens' she had asked when I had left, thinking that I had taken several days for the journey. Her astonishment that anybody could cycle eighty five miles in a day was shared by all in the bar, to whom she announced the news in tones of wonder. I felt a little self-conscious. I knew that my daily total would not be considered large within the cycling world. I hoped that there were no other cyclists in the bar.

In truth, I was a little disappointed to discover that I had only cycled eighty five miles. On the day before, my journey from Arras to Amiens had been a shade over fifty miles. Even though I had been weary at the end of it, I had been certain that I could have cycled up to a hundred had I needed to. How deceptive stamina can be! Never could I have cycled another fifteen miles last night to have reached the total of one hundred miles: the total which I arbitrarily considered myself capable of.

I had seen Montreuil on the way into France and could think of no reason why I should grace it with a second appearance so I struck out across country towards the coast. I had, as usual, chosen a minor road which actually was the most direct route to the coast from my point of departure.

When I was half way to my goal, it became obvious that I was not the only person thereabouts who had realised that this cross country route was useful, for the road suddenly opened out into broad tarmac. There was not much that I could do about it. To make myself feel better, when I reached Rang du Fliers, I cycled down a gravelly track which sneaked away between two buildings opposite the station. To my trained eye, it was obviously an old railway track. Probably part of a seaside steam tramway system that had long since perished.

Behind a pair of modern warehouses, the track disappeared into a vault of trees and became a pretty country footpath. I was enchanted. Despite the heat, under those trees the earth was still damp, the foliage, humid and the air hung pungent with odours of a sleepy wood which was loath to awaken.

When I arrived at the recently erected steel footbridge which crossed the drainage ditch full of green water, I laid down my bicycle and inspected the abutments. They were of brick, old brick, and the four girders upon which the footbridge had been laid were of equal vintage. The bridge which had originally stood here had been constructed to carry locomotives.

It is so nice for one's hypotheses to be proven correct in such a positive manner – and so rare! As if to crush any dissenters to my theory, a few hundred yards further along where the track joined a road, the sign told me that the street was called *impasse de l'arret*, indicating that at some time it must have led to a railway halt.

I straddled my crossbar, looked down the track and squinted. I could imagine a busy little steam engine with a tall chimney pompously chuffing a couple of open-sided wooden carriages away from the front yard of the main line station and then whistling cheekily as it crossed the road. I could see the bright eyed families, miners from the nearby northern coalfields, rocking and rattling with the train as it truckled them to their *pension* for their annual holiday at the seaside. They would be going to Berck-sur-Mer just as they still do today.

I have always liked Berck. Someone has to. It needs friends with a name sounding as it does. Berck! That is the French equivalent of the noise a rude person would make when presented with an unappetising dish. But I have other reasons for liking Berck.

For a start, it is not conceited like its neighbouring Le Touquet Paris Plage. It does not intimidate you with winding approach roads through a forest, or avenues lined by expensive detached houses. Secondly, it is not dishonest like Montreuil-sur-Mer. When Berck says it is '*sur mer*' it jolly well is. You don't have to stand on top of the wardrobe with a telescope to confirm the claim. And thirdly, it is not full of English people. That was an unkind remark to make but admit it; be honest with yourselves. When you are on holiday in France, do you seek out the company of your compatriots? Are you unreservedly proud of their comportment? No? Well now you see why I like Berck.

Berck is where the French go for a seaside holiday. Its sandy hinterland is peppered with campsites ranging from the downright awful to the upright exorbitant. It does not have the veneer of 'Paris Plage'. It is stripped of pretension. The town starts immediately behind the promenade so that you can find a hotel which is a few yards from the sea, the cafés and the shops.

Pride of place has to go to the beach. It is the beach which is the jewel of Berck. In summer, the tide never reaches up to the promenade and so the first thirty yards of sand are hot, dry and sifted like Saxa salt. The sand invites you to kick off your sandals and allow it to trickle through your toes. It is the nearest element to a liquid whilst remaining a solid. It is gorgeous!

As you progress down the flat beach you pass the volley ball nets and the beach play club for the children. The sand here is firmer but dries quickly as the tide recedes. Keep walking. When you are about four hundred yards from the promenade and still walking on sand, you arrive at a narrow depression which runs parallel to the sea front for the length of the visible beach.

You descend the bank, it is only about four or five feet lower than the rest of the beach and you splish splash through the shallow water that has been trapped here as the tide ebbed. It is deliciously warm and speckled with little shrimps and children in equal numbers. This is the *'bache'* as it is known in local patois. It is a line of depressions in the sand caused by the outflow of springs on the beach which are then driven along in a direction parallel to the sea by the dominant wind. It is open at the northern end and it is through this breach that the trapped water slowly drains. In the interim it provides a snug and safe bathing area for the young children where they can float on inflatable toys with no risk of taking to the high seas and where they can jump and splash to their content whilst remaining under the eyes of their watchful parents.

Cross the *bache*, climb up the other side and continue walking, for the sea is still five hundred yards away at low tide. The broad rollers thunder in menacingly and then subside with the magic of the steps of an escalator, leaving a foaming lace tablecloth being shaken after Sunday lunch. A little way from the surf's edge, a rubber boat is buzzing back and forth, shepherding the swimmers, preventing them from attempting to walk to Kent which from this gently sloping beach does not seem impossible.

When I first stayed in Berck, years earlier, I was told about the *baches* and about how they quickly filled up when the tide rose and I was determined to see such a phenomenon. If only because my enticer had not breathed a word of foam-flecked galloping horses, which I could only mark to his credit. But time and tide wait for no man. I came almost to the end of my short sojourn without having coincided my presence with the rising tide and yet, such a meeting should have been easy to arrange since one side of the party was reliably consistent in its movements. This shows what a poor organiser I am.

Eventually, my last evening saw me trudging down the beach at half past ten at night to keep an appointment to meet the rising tide, or so I hoped. I had not taken a torch since there was nothing for me to encounter, no rocks, no wrecks, no kerbs. The light from the promenade glinted on the soft undulations and threw a ghostly sheen on the hard-packed flat sand which made it appear to glow from within.

I ambled on into the blackness, outside the arc of the lamps. It was unreal to be walking into the deepening gloom. I stopped and turned. The promenade was now just a thin silver snake.

Then a magical incident occurred. It was summer. A quarter of a mile away stretched the facade of Berck. The lights of the seafront apartment blocks twinkled in the balmy night and from them, across the sand to me, came the beginning of a sound. It was a hiss which grew in volume as if an army of asthmatics were taking a deep breath in unison. Then it suddenly stopped and was succeeded by a roar which gained quickly in volume to end in a rumbling cheer of delight, half a mile wide. I was stunned. As I stood there, my mouth agape, the cheer slowly subsided and with its diminution I identified its cause.

France had just scored a goal.

I now remembered why my host had been unwilling to accompany me on my mad wanderings – he wanted to stay in to see *le match*. France versus Spain. European cup football. And along the sea front, in every apartment, on every balcony, the Berckois were watching the match on their televisions. And the windows were open. What I had heard was the population of Berck drawing in a breath and cheering its country's goal.

I don't know how the match ended because I am not the least interested in football. No doubt my host told me the score upon my return. I have never been to a football match, but I will never forget that unseen goal. I had experienced something that I was never likely to enjoy again either by design or desire.

I turned and walked on. I was now in a sort of marginal limbo. I could no longer hear the town, I could not yet hear the sea.

When I reached the *bache* I wisely chose not to cross it. I could barely distinguish a slight reflection rippling in the residue of light radiating from the town far behind me. I stopped and waited. I felt rather foolish and was glad that I was alone. It was ten minutes to eleven and although the tide should by now have been on the turn, I could still not hear the sea. The only noise I could detect was a strange popping and sucking exuding from the wet sand at my feet. I attributed this to lugworm or whatever the beasties are that live in the sand.

I stood and waited, straining my eyes and ears as I looked to my right and left – still nothing. I concentrated on the dim definition of the sand before me, noting landmarks such as worm casts and shells. Just at the limit of my vision, about fifteen feet away, I could see the dark line of a stick and I decided that it would be a good idea to use it as a marker so I started towards it but I need not have bothered because it appeared to be moving towards me.

When it was about four feet distant, I recognised it for what it was. A tiny ripple of water. I laughed derisively as it reached my shoe and I took a step backwards. The ripple continued unabashed. I moved the other foot, it carried on and slapped against my shoe with more force than I had expected. A bit surprised, but still mocking, I skipped playfully backwards and then noticed that to my right the water was foaming white. Indeed, when I turned around I discovered that the sea had stealthily reached about six feet behind me on one side. I appeared to be standing on a little spit of sand, slightly higher than the surrounding beach. I was brought to my senses by a cupful of cold water tipping over the heel and into the back of my shoe. At last, seeing the situation in its true light, I walked briskly back up my spit which was narrowing by the second. I reached the main portion of the beach just as the two waves clapped together and covered my spur.

I could not be certain that all the beach that I had crossed so far on my trek to the water had been of a uniform gradient so I marched smartly towards the promenade hoping that I would not come across a foaming torrent barring my path.

Well, I obviously did not drown. When I returned to my host's flat he cast a sardonic eye over me.

'You appear to have got your feet wet. Did it catch you by surprise?'

'Not a bit of it. I merely felt that I should, after all, christen myself in the Channel. *Noblesse oblige* and all that.'

So I had a reason to go to Berck today. Not only because I liked the town but because I intended, once and for all, to actually witness the filling of the *baches* in daylight. Without getting my shoes wet. The question was, would the tide play ball, as it were?

I locked my machine against the hot railings of the promenade and, rashly suppressing my feeling that I was overdressed in a tee shirt and shorts, I fixed my eyes on the blue foaming margin and marched towards it. But I could not resist that sand and quickly I pulled off my shoes, stuffed them with my socks and wriggled my toes through the baking grains like miniature maize harvesters. There were many people on the beach, all conversing fluidly in International Beach Body Language. One day I would amuse myself by writing a manual for it but at the moment, I had an appointment.

I stood on the lip of the *bache* and gazed benevolently upon the naked, dripping children who were scratching about in the few inches of muddy water. This was encouraging for if the level of the water in the *bache* had fallen so much then the tide must be on the turn. I could see the rollers crashing into the sand approximately three hundred yards beyond. From where I stood I could hear the shrieks and shouts of the bathers as they were thrown up and down in the rumbustious surf, tumbling like corks in a washing machine.

A few yards out, the rescue boat was grumbling back and forth, edging the bathers back towards the beach. A lifeguard, standing at the margin, blew an urgent note on a battered brass bugle and signalled to a swimmer that he was too far out. This was the area of the beach which was 'supervised bathing' and the lifeguards appeared to be bent on disrupting everybody's enjoyment.

In a peacock's tail of spray, a Land Rover bounced down the beach, towing a boat-trailer and soon another rescue boat was rumbling out to dance with the other, nudging the bathers inexorably in to the beach. Some of them were now walking back to me over the bank of sand towards the *bache*. I presumed that the harassment by the lifeguards had finally dissuaded them from their games. A couple of parents brushed past me and shouted to their offspring, playing in the warm water.

'David, Crystale, Come quickly! The tide's coming in. Come on!'

Two urchins shrugged their little shoulders and wailed something back at their parents but nevertheless they clambered out of the water. Was it my imagination or was the water in the *bache* a little deeper? It was deeper and it was swirling. More parents came to the edge and dragged recalcitrant children out. I realised then what the danger was. The tide was rising and although the sea was still a hundred yards away, the *bache* was below the level of the tide and of course it was open at the northern end. It was through this aperture that the tide was now rushing in a torrent. On the opposite bank an elaborate dock and castle suddenly slid into the water to the utter dismay of its architect and chief contractor but he was soon scooped up by his father who had waded across to retrieve him. Out in the surf, a few bathers were still leaping up and down with the fast approaching tide. Did they realise that it was rising behind them, leaving them upon a sandbank?

The water was now foaming and frothing as it ran through the gulley with the power of a tidal race. It was a foot deep and I moved back from the brink because I was hindering the serious migration that was now taking place. A few diehards or fools remained where they were. The sea was now only twenty yards from the *bache* and one or two of the returning bathers registered surprise on their faces as they crossed the swirling stream and the water snatched powerfully at their waists.

I waited until the sea finally tipped over the rim into the

perilous trough and then I ambled back up towards the promenade with the others. We were like a crowd of failed lemmings. I was gingerly unlocking my bicycle from the barbecued metal railings when the ambulance arrived.

'Another drowning,' I heard a passer-by remark. 'That makes three this month.'

chapter eight

Weaving slowly between the holiday cars which were snuffling along the sea front, I began to look for somewhere to eat. Reaching the sea had exerted a strange influence over me. Just as I recognised at Amiens that I was turning for home, arriving at the sea made the end of my journey seem uncomfortably close. Although I did not intend to go home until the morrow, it was inescapably obvious to me that I was now only three hours ride from Boulogne. I could easily get home tonight if I wanted to. If I did not go home this evening then where would I stay overnight? It would be ridiculous to pay for a hotel in Boulogne and then take a boat in the morning. Similarly, it would be pointless to stop cycling at midday today just to leave me some kilometres to cycle tomorrow. Too late I realised my mistake. I had reached the sea too early. I should not have come in sight of it until tomorrow, after lunch, but now I had seen it, it was irrevocably drawing me home.

Berck is famous in the medical world for its treatment of bone disorders, especially in children and the patients are often seen in the streets, propelling themselves along in wheelchairs or some even in a sort of reclining chair more reminiscent of the bath chairs of olden times. They move in and out of the traffic quite confidently and I was happy to see that they were not jostled or intimidated. Perhaps Berck realised that it owed its prosperity not only to tourism but also to the successful functioning of the *Hopital Maritime* and the *Hopital Rothschild* and the many miscellaneous smaller clinics that are dispersed in the town.

I cycled alongside a mock gothic building which vaguely resembled a market building or some such establishment. A necklace of buses was arranged untidily on the scrubby grass behind it and above this facade hung a sign: *'Gare Routiere'* – the bus station. How preposterous! It was plain to all with eyes in their heads and not in their pockets that this was the former railway station. The train whose track I had discovered earlier would have come down that road *there*, following that curve to the platform which would have been just *here*. Then it would have continued on down that road towards the dunes and Le Touquet. I wonder if it ever reached Le Touquet? I would look it up when I got home tonight.

Then I realised that I had said it. 'When I get home tonight'. I resigned myself to good sense. I would go home tonight. In the meantime, I would eat somewhere. I will eat right *here*. I can be a man of decision when I want to be, you know. No vacillation, straight in with a resolution.

I was the first customer and chose a table well in to the interior away from the glare of the sun on the sandy streets. A young man of obvious North African parentage left me with the menu. He left me for about fifteen minutes. Perhaps he thought that I was a slow reader. He eventually reappeared from behind the glass screen by the kitchen and took my order. Several more customers drifted in and sat around the room, a couple here, a foursome there, a man on his own by the hat stand. To each one the waiter delivered a menu and from each one he took an order.

We sat and looked at each other discreetly. The talking was mumbled. Twenty minutes later we were still sitting and looking at each other, nothing having occurred in the interim. No hors d'oeuvres had been produced, no bread had been distributed, no drinks delivered. It is often said that we English do not know how to complain and that is why we endure such terrible service. I am archetypically English in this matter. I made myself excuses; thirty five minutes was not too long to wait; one should not rush food; nobody else had been served so I could not think that I had been unfairly treated.

Astonishingly, the French seemed to be doing the same, for nobody said a word. We had been sitting there for thirty five minutes, eight of us. We had given our orders to the man who had been very civil and had then secreted himself behind the glass screen. He could have been half way back to Rabat for all we knew.

I argued with myself to establish the best course of action. I could hardly complain on my own and yet, I had been here for fifteen minutes longer than anybody else so, in theory, the resonsibility for action rested upon my shoulders as the doyen of our little diplomatic enclave.

The situation reminded me of an incident which had occurred in a modest restaurant in my quarter of Paris many years earlier. I had lived in a respectable area. Not a brashly rich and prosperous nor an indulgently Latin and Apache district, just a solid, reliable, go-to-church-on-Sundays area. This sedateness was reflected in the mirrors which decorated one long wall of the rectangular dining room. The only other embellishment was to be found in the art nouveau flourishes on the globe candelabra. The rest was straightforward. Three lines of chairs and tables, street door at one end, service door at the other end and that was it. The food was in the same measure as the restaurant – unfussy and uncomplicated.

I ate there occasionally, perhaps once a fortnight. I would have eaten there more often but there was a question of my awkward working hours not being compatible with its restricted opening hours. This particular evening, I was halfway through my first course when the street door opened and a man shuffled in. At first glance I thought that he was a tramp. His long grey hair lay untidily over his coat collar and he was carrying something coarsely wrapped up in newspaper.

My split second assessment of this man was obviously shared by the waitress who flew down the aisle towards him whilst drawing herself up into the stratosphere of haughtiness.

'What do you want?' she asked him whilst barring his progress into the *salle*. From the man's weather-burned face a pair of blue eyes twinkled back at her.

'To eat,' he replied with mischief in his voice and he sat at the nearest table before she could prevent him. She pinched her lips and watched him silently as he carefully placed his newspaper package on the chair beside him then she spun around and marched back up to the cash desk. I could hear fragments of a discussion with another woman who remained out of sight behind the door. I heard the word 'dirty' and 'tramp' a couple of times.

Between them they established a strategy and wheeled it into action. The waitress sallied forth.

'What do you want to eat?'

'What is there?'

She sighed heavily and insolently looked at the ceiling. She snatched up the menu card from the table behind her and thrust it at the man. He peered at it.

'What is that?' he asked.

'What there is to eat,' the woman replied, not very precisely. The man took the card and turned it over slowly.

'I'm not eating that! Haven't you got any food?'

I sniggered into my soup but was harpooned by a glare from the waitress. Those customers who were not trying to prove that they were the most interesting and important people south of the Seine were also watching but they had the sense to laugh behind their napkins.

'You read what is on it,' she instructed through a mouth shaped like a cigar tube.

'I don't want something to read, I want something to eat. I go to a book shop when I want something to read.'

'Do you want anything to eat or don't you, because I have got better things–?'

'Omelette!'

'What?'

'Omelette. I'll have an omelette. You know how to do that do you?'

'Omelette?' she confirmed.

'It's made with eggs. You beat them up and–'

'Yes I know, I know. Drink?'

He looked her in the face and sucked his top lip. She tapped her foot impatiently on the floor. He scratched his nose.

'Do you have wine?'

'Red or white?'

'Which have you got?'

'Which do you want?'

'The one you have.'

'We have both.'

'Oh I don't want both.'

'A glass of red wine,' she decreed and snatched up the menu.

'A pichet?' he suggested with a hint of a wheedle in his voice.

'Not with an omelette. A glass.'

He shrugged and she stormed back up the aisle, hissing through her teeth. Again I caught snippets of a discussion behind me. 'Only two eggs, no more,' and then, 'Not that wine, this one. Take the small glass.'

He finished his minute meal and single glass of wine long before I had finished my repast. He sat there, gazing around at the lights, the bustle and the movement rather as I imagined somebody newly released from prison would do. Occasionally he mysteriously unwrapped a corner of his package and peered down the funnel of newspaper and then unerringly looked quickly up to catch the stare of the intrigued diners who in their turn were eaten up with curiosity. This seemed to amuse him and his eyes twinkled with more mischief.

He made several attempts to attract the attention of the waitress but she wanted nothing to do with him. She refused even to look in his direction, sweeping her eyes over him without registering his presence.

I was slowly demolishing a creme caramel when the next scene in the evening's drama unfurled. The waitress was performing a delicate silver service involving a tureen and some large spoons which she held like tongs. Something distracted her and she glanced up and exclaimed angrily.

'Ah ça, non!'

She smacked the serving dishes rudely down onto an adjacent empty table, quickstepped round the chairs and tables to the street door and grabbed the man by his coat sleeve.

'Come back monsieur, you have forgotten to pay.'

He turned to look at her with raised eyebrows as if an injustice were being perpetrated upon him. It was a masterly pose. He, nevertheless, allowed himself to be drawn quietly back into the restaurant where he resumed his former place. But by this time the clientele of the entire restaurant was aware of the situation.

'But I cannot pay, madame,' he admitted simply.

'Ha! I knew it! I knew it!' The splintery light of vindication spat from her eyes in shards. 'The moment you walked in the door I knew it. You're nothing but a tramp.

(to the kitchen) Mme Hogarth! (to the salle) Oh yes. Just to look at you. Well you're a thief and a (to the kitchen) Madame Hogarth! (to the salle) we have had enough of people like you. We are not a charity. This is not the *Assistance Publique*. I work my fingers to the bone, every evening...' A dour woman in black had waddled down the restaurant towards them. 'Madame Hogarth. I gave him what you said and then I caught him trying to sneak out without paying. I was serving...' She looked up the aisle to where the two customers were guiltily spooning food from the steaming serving dishes rather than allowing it to cool. They grinned self consciously.

'You permit us?'

'Go ahead. Help yourselves!' the waitress replied magnanimously.

Madame Hogarth looked at the man and then said grandly, 'Emilie, telephone the Commissariat.'

On her triumphant march to the telephone, Emilie the waitress harangued the gods and the customers declaring the accuracy of her percipience and the rectitude of her actions.

The Commissariat was only two short streets away and Madame Hogarth stood fidgeting by the door, watching for the policemen. Emilie attempted to recoup the delay in serving her customers. I decided that I could wait for my coffee. Only the cause of all the fuss appeared in any way serene. He cast his blue eyes around us all, grinning benevolently, as if he had just made a great joke.

The policeman obviously knew Madame Hogarth. They shook hands and exchanged a few general sentences before turning to the problem, who beamed up at them.

'Now, Madame Hogarth said that she caught you leaving without paying. Is that so?'

'Not true.' He raised a finger to make the precise point. 'It was the other dragon who caught me.'

A titter ran around the room until Madame Hogarth

choked it with a stare. It was fortunate that she had looked away because from the contortions on the policeman's face, it was obvious to me that he was having trouble suppressing a smile.

'Now you'll see what the police will do, you thief! They will lock you up!' the waitress snarled.

The last thing that the policeman wanted was to have to escort this tramp back to the station and lock him up for the night. I immediately recognised a conflict of interests which could be summed up thus: Madame Hogarth wanted her money, Emilie wanted retribution and the policeman wanted a quiet evening. The man grinned from one to the other. I think he knew very well what he wanted.

'When Em... the waitress stopped you from leaving and asked you to pay, you refused. Is that correct?'

'I said that I could not pay.'

'You know, it is wrong to go into a shop and take things without paying don't you?' The man nodded. 'It is simply stealing. If you come into a restaurant and eat food, knowing that you could not pay, that is a particularly mean sort of stealing isn't it? Because the proprietor cannot recover his goods.'

'I agree. But I did not know when I came in that I would be unable to pay.'

The policeman looked at him, visibly measuring him up. Neither man was a fool and they respected each other in the game that they were playing even though, as the guardian of the law realised, the game was weighted to one side and the final score was predictable.

'If you thought that you were able to pay when you came in why can you not pay now?'

'He's got no money, that's why!' Emilie accused him shrilly. The policeman held up his hand.

'Because...' the man began slowly, making sure that everybody was listening, 'because I have got no... bill.'

'You have got no bill? Can this be true?' The policeman's

surprise was evident in the tone of his voice.

'I tried several times to get one... but I was... not seen,' he explained modestly.

'Bah... Madame...' Emilie shrugged her excuse to Madame Hogarth.

'We will rectify that now. Emilie, give this customer his bill. Then we will see if he will pay.'

'With pleasure madame.'

Playing his audience, keeping them on tenterhooks the man gave a great show of comparing the bill to the menu.

'I don't think this is correct,' he said at length.

'Have you got the money or haven't you?' Madame Hogarth snapped.

The man looked up at her with the hurt look in his eyes and then continued. 'You have charged me for the *'menu omelette'* which is three eggs. There were not three eggs in my omelette were there madame?'

She said nothing but snatched away the scrap of paper and scribbled on it,

'Satisfied?' She tapped her pencil on the table cloth. 'He hasn't got any money, He's wasting our time. Why don't you take him away now?'

'I could hardly do it without giving him a chance of paying you madame,' the policeman explained with a measured civility.

The man began to look in his coat pocket then, knowing that all eyes were upon him, he stopped and pointedly looked from his table to the adjoining table and then back again.

'Would you be so kind,' he asked of the policeman, 'to hand me that glass?'

The policeman handed him the glass. He placed it next to his empty wine glass and ostentatiously lowering his head, compared the two.

'The wine seems to have shrunk my glass. Unless of course...'

Madame Hogarth was now purple in the face as she snatched back the scrap of paper and amended it yet again. She slapped it down before him.

'Now let's see your money!'

He inclined his head in submission and put his hand into his coat pocket. A puzzled frown creased his face. He searched in another pocket as his consternation increased.

'Well?' she snapped.

'I would request you respectfully to be patient madame. I have only just received my bill.'

I was enthralled by the entire performance, as were the diners. Not a sound was heard, not a cough, not a spoon dropped as all ears and eyes were tuned to the drama being played out before us. This was better than the Comédie Française. He had his audience on the palm of his hand.

With a sigh he withdrew a battered leather wallet from his jacket pocket. Madame Hogarth barely restrained herself from snatching it from him. The slight movement that she made did not go unnoticed and he turned it to his use mercilessly.

'Ah ha. madame. This is MY wallet and in any case...' He opened it before her. '...it has no money in it. Never keep money in your wallet madame. Take my advice. A thief will always go for your wallet but will rarely look in one's shirt pocket.' He pulled out a folded scrap of paper and dropped it onto the bill. 'You have change I hope?'

Like a pair of squabbling starlings, the two women descended on the scrap of paper and tore it open. It was a Bank of France currency note to the value of five hundred francs. Thirty times the value of the meal.

'Ah you think that is funny do you?' she threw at him as she waddled back up the restaurant towards the till, 'wasting the time of good honest workers.'

I thought that she was going a bit far applying that epithet to herself, given the exposé we had all just enjoyed over the omelette and the wine but I was still waiting for my coffee so I said nothing. Whilst they were mumbling at the till the man stood up and slowly unwrapped the newspaper from his parcel to show the policeman. Customers craned their necks to see the object and a murmur of delight ran around the room. It was a beautiful translucent blue and green glass art deco statuette. The policeman was in a quandary. He must have immediately thought that the man had stolen it but something in the way that he handled it, that he caressed its curves, made that suspicion untenable.

'It's Lalique crystal. I recognise that,' the policeman declared proudly. 'It must be worth a fortune.'

'Ah my friend, that is where you are wrong. I have not the imagination of Lalique. It is not original. I can only copy what I am paid to copy.'

The policeman stood aghast.

'Did you make it?'

'It took me four months. It is to replace one of a pair that was unfortunately broken by a domestic servant.'

'Aren't you frightened of dropping it?' He was horrified.

'Yes,' the man replied simply. 'I am.'

My mind was jerked away from the luscious crystal by the waitress who asked me quietly, 'Would you monsieur, have change for a five hundred franc note?'

I did not. And even if I had, I would have said that I had not. To Madame Hogarth's shame, she had to borrow one hundred francs from the policeman. The glass sculptor carefully re-enrobed the statuette in its crumpled *Paris Soir* and as he left with the policeman he said quietly to nobody in particular but so that everybody heard,

'You see madame, the mistake we made was to judge by appearances. We both did it. The only difference was that my judgment was correct from the first.'

All this happened a long time ago and I only recounted it to fill in the time whilst I waited for my lunch but after forty five minutes I decided that enough was enough. Although it was probably too late to get into another restaurant, if I just got up and walked out I could buy myself something to eat in the supermarket. Bread and sardines or some such nourishment. I had my hands on the edge of the table ready to rise when another North African entered. He walked straight to the glass screen and shook hands with the waiter who had magically materialised. They babbled and bubbled, expectorated and scratched in an Arabic tongue of sorts. Then the new arrival inspected the order slips laid out on the narrow shelf and wandered gently through into the kitchen. The cook had arrived!

The main road back to Boulogne via Etaples and Neufchatel Hardelot was unremarkable. It was perfectly flat as far as Etaples but once across the cobbled bridge it ran up and down like the seam on a hospital eiderdown. I felt strangely flat myself. I had lost my driving force. It was not physical tiredness that had overcome me but a mental torpor which brought with it the paradoxical argument: why go on? – you are nearly home.

I did not know, as my weary wheels rolled me back to Boulogne, that this excursion into France, which was the first for me, was to become the first of many. I did not know that in a few years hence I would be on nodding terms with every pothole and café along the length of this road. I could not recognise this patch of sand which was where I was to upend my bike one evening when racing back for the ferry, take off both wheels, change the good front tyre with the rear, mend a puncture and still reach the port in time for the boat. This kerb appeared undistinguished from any other and yet it was to break my rib at the start of a cycling trip to Paris with Frank and Hairy. The striped blind of the bistrot jogged my memory not one jot although this estaminet was destined to be where we would snuggle around cups of steaming hot chocolate whilst sheltering from the pouring summer rain, only to find the sky blue and the black road steaming when we came out again.

This patisserie was where I was to buy a *chausson aux pommes* with my last three francs and then drop it into the dirty gutter before I could eat it.

Fate had decided to keep me in ignorance of the multifarious roles that all these places must at that very moment have been quietly practising behind the scenes. These rehearsals were in order for them to perform their parts in the farce of my life which they were to do with such faultless timing on every subsequent occasion when I spun a pedal in France. In my subjective myopia, I could only see the road and my opinion of the road was that it was quite bland and carried far too much holiday traffic ever to endear itself to me.

Sitting in the gently vibrating bar of the homeward bound ferry, I thoughtfully sipped my tepid grapefruit juice and reflected that, all in all, by and large, all things being equal and other meaningless expressions, I had had a good time. Parenthetically, I can recommend grapefruit juice if you want a long drink. It is ghastly and so you can only sip it and wait until its revolting taste is no more a memory before resipping. In this manner, the drink lasts for ages. An insoluble problem is what to do with the final mouthful. I really believe that every person ordering a grapefruit juice should be entitled to a glass of water to wash away the taste at the end.

'Crew announcement. Carpenter to the bridge please, carpenter to the bridge.'

I jumped in alarm, recalling my outward journey and the insistent explanations of the sandy-haired man who had latched on to me. I found myself to be discreetly examining all the faces in the bar to give me early warning of an accosting. Then I laughed at myself for being so stupid. What a teeth-grinding bore that man had been! Fancy him believing that he could fool me with all that claptrap! And he had pronounced it with such earnestness that one could not doubt that he believed it himself. I took a swig at my grapefruit juice and simultaneously received a blow in the back.

'Sorry sir. Didn't see you standing in front of the door,' the steward apologised and swung his coffee tray deftly to the other hand. He pushed the service door closed behind him with his foot and then, whistling nonchalantly, he sauntered off towards the bridge.

There are times when it is better not to draw any conclusions.

chapter nine

So why had I enjoyed my trip so much? It had been hard work. Some of the hills had been unwelcome and a mite too enthusiastic in their perpendicularity. I had not laughed all the way. Underlying every day's journey had been the tension of not knowing whether or not there would be a hotel at the end of it and even when the hotel was found, I was still unsure as to whether or not I had chosen the most appropriate. Several times I had found myself gnashing my teeth in frustration. I had sometimes waited far too long for my meals and frankly, I would have preferred to have been able to spend more money. So why had I enjoyed my trip so much?

As I whirred up the loading ramp onto the soil at Folkestone, why was my sun-pinked face all abeam with contentment? It was the achievement. It was because I had done it, quite simply that. I had taken a bike to France and pedalled around for five days. I had gone where I had wanted, when I had wanted, how I had wanted. If the fancy had taken me to stop and look at a cow, I had done just that. Nobody had been there to question my motives or demand conclusions. When I had wanted solitude it had been there. If I had wanted company, it had been easily found. If I had made a mistake, I had suffered but had not been held responsible for the suffering of others. I have to explain this to you for you to understand the irony of what happened next.

I was on the pinnacle of enthusiasm and like many small-minded people when they first achieve a mediocre goal, I could not prevent myself from talking about it to everybody I met. I do feel that I might just have been a teeny weeny bit boring but you will be pleased to learn that I received my comeuppance in a horribly appropriate manner.

Hairy listened attentively to my exhortations to solo Continental adventure and then asked, 'Are you going again next year?'

'You bet!' I affirmed.

'Good, then I'll come with you. You make it sound like real fun.'

I was lost for words. The central reason for it having been 'real fun' was that I had been on my own. If Hairy came with me, all that would be lost I was certain. I stalled, I tried unkindly to think of excuses or stratagems to prevent him from coming, but failed.

Then I received my second blow. Frank said that he wanted to come as well – it would make a change from Suffolk. I became frantic. I didn't dare open my mouth on the subject of cycling for fear that some other volunteer would throw himself under my wheels. I would awaken, screaming at night, tortured by visions of me pedalling demoniacally across the plains of Artois, pursued like the Pied Piper, by a streamer of acquaintances chanting, 'You make it sound like real fun.'

I gave in. I had to. There was no other way. I only had myself to blame. Be positive! Just think of the pleasure you will have, showing Frank and Hairy the deserted French roads, the quaint little cafés, the cemeteries. Well, perhaps not the cemeteries.

Of course there would have to be no pushing cars up hills or getting stuck in phone boxes – none of that palaver. And just to be completely safe, we would not go within twenty miles of Hesdin.

I have an overdue revelation to make. It is that of the identities of Frank and Hairy. In an opus such as this, it is obviously undesirable to divulge the real names of the main participants. Apart from the rather sordid self-agrandissement aspect there is the not inconsiderable possibility of court action to bear in mind.

There are several ways of solving this problem. One trick is to start the work with the classic and well-worn disclaimer about there being 'no intended similarity to any persons living or dead'. I don't like that formula, it implies that the people described bear no relation to the human race at all or are zombies and it can only serve as an utter discouragement to the prospective reader.

Another tactic is to give your characters pseudonyms. The problem with this, is that if the circumstances you portrayed in the account supply sufficient information to enable the reader to identify the real people, then the latter can still sue you for every groat in the mattress.

I thought long and hard about this dilemma and came up with a solution so simple and effective that even I was astonished at my audacity. If I call the characters, 'Frank' and 'Hairy', no reader worth his bookmark will believe that I know anybody with such names. So if I then catalogue the exploits of these two, as they happen, then the reader will be content to accept the account as an obvious work of imaginative fiction. So Frank and Hairy (real names) actually did and said all the things that I shall describe. But of course, you will not believe me so I am quite safe.

As I was forced more and more to accept the dreadful inevitability of my being accompanied on my next voyage, I began to pepper my preparations with investigations and tests designed to discover and assess our compatibility. I came upon one sticking point – Frank. Hairy, I had known for far longer than Frank and so we had already established our mutual antagonism. As for Frank, whilst I recognised his unarguable prowess with anything mechanical, I had yet to be convinced that the marriage of our minds would bring nothing but harmony. In short, were we on the same wavelength or at least, in the same spectrum?

Robert was to be the unintentional catalyst in my research. For several years Robert had been organising, in the loosest meaning of the word, a monthly ride for acquaintances. The supposed format was that we would choose a Wednesday, usually the first in the month, and meet outside a pub at about nine thirty. From there we would amble gently around the countryside, stopping for morning coffee somewhere en route until we found another pub for lunch. After this, we would gradually split up onto our divergent routes homeward.

What actually happened was something rather different. Robert is what I would call a 'bum-in-the-air-merchant'. Cycling is one of the rare forms of strenuous exercise that you can actually enjoy from a sedentary position and I think that it might have been this quality which subconsciously attracted me to it. As far as Robert is concerned, cycling is about getting to where you want to go so that you do not see anything en route and arrive covered in sweat.

Off we go at a gentle pace but before long he yields to temptation; his nose goes onto the front tyre, his posterior is hoisted heavenwards and he disappears off around the corner at ninety miles per hour. At first, I used to keep up with him but I soon realised the futility of the operation for we always arrived at the pub together so what was the advantage? Also, it was far too much like hard work.

Towards the end of the morning he would usually say something like, 'there's a nice little café in the next village where we can have coffee.' In all fairness, he had a vast and detailed knowledge of the county, of the byroads and the watering places. This permitted him to lead the group with a fluidity of movement which we all envied. He never carried a map but always knew where we were and where we should go next, so it was a great pity that the cafés were always closed when we got to them. It became a standing joke – *'Robert's Cycling Guide to the Cafés Which Always Close on Wednesdays'*. When they weren't closed they had changed into ironmongers' shops, furniture stores or something similar; the transmogrification having been accomplished within the rising and setting of one moon, if we were to believe Robert.

On this particular ride, at two o'clock, we were cosily ensconced in an isolated pub, perched in a windswept corner of Kent and toasting our toes over a log fire. We had polished off our meals with gusto and were now warming our hands around coffee cups. Occasionally the window rattled urgently and the wind moaned eerily around the casement. Frank glanced at it.

'It's weird isn't it, this Kentish fixation with cosy fields and draughty houses?'

'Um,' I said.

Robert was braver, he asked, 'What do you mean?'

'Think of the last five miles that we rode to get here. Every field was surrounded by a twenty foot high poplar hedge planted for a windbreak to keep the apple trees or mangelwurzels warm and yet this house is unprotected on all sides. That wind is blowing directly from the Arctic and the first thing that it hits is the north wall of this pub.'

'Oh yes,' Robert agreed, with, I thought, a distinct lack of enthusiasm.

'What always amuses me with windbreaks,' I began, 'is that you plant them as windbreaks but you would be considerably annoyed if they spent their time doing just that.'

Frank grinned. Robert looked puzzled.

'I don't get you,' he said.

'Imagine lying in bed of a winter's night, trying vainly to get to sleep to the sound of the forty two poplar trees which surround your house, all breaking wind.'

Frank's explanation was sonorous and I joined him in a boisterous orchestration until my lips tingled with the vibration and my chin ran with saliva.

'Are you all right gents?' The landlord poked a wary head through the hatchway.

We settled down. Robert wriggled. It was probably his shorts chafing him.

'Talking of altered dimensions–' I began.

'We weren't,' Robert interrupted. He can be a bit of a pedant at times.

'–you know that map of the British Isles which is pinned up above the filing cabinet in the clerk's room at work?' They nodded assent. 'Well, I was looking at it for some time before I realised what was wrong with it.'

'It was upside down?' Frank suggested.

I ignored him.

'No, in order to get it all on one sheet, they had pushed Ireland right in close against Wales. They had altered the grid all right but even so, not many people automatically refer to the grid.'

'It probably shortens the Holyhead ferry crossing by a couple of hours,' Frank observed. He had a practical streak in him. Robert decided that the topic of conversation was not worth the breath. Despite Robert's discouraging glance, Frank persisted obstinately. 'I always find worrying this inability of cartographers to accept that the land is that shape however awkward it might be to put on paper. Especially the Orkneys and the Shetlands.'

'Yes, they do get shunted about a bit, don't they?'

'You usually find them in a white box somewhere off Grimsby.'

'Wouldn't it be funny....' I half proposed. Robert began to drum his fingers on the table and purse his lips. '...if they really did turn up there?'

'You're being ridiculous.' Robert vainly tried to stop the conversation before it ran amok but Frank adopted the concept with alacrity.

'Yes. Imagine some salt-stained trawler, fumbling out of Grimsby. Chaos on the bridge:

'White line ahead cap'n'.

'White line? What do you mean, "White line"?'

'Take a look for yourself cap'n.'

'You're right bo'sun. It's a white line and if I'm not mistaken, that's Lerwick that I can see on the other side. That shouldn't be there!'

'Beg pardon cap'n, but look at the map. You see, down in the right hand corner – "The Shetland Isles".'

'Egad bosun! You're right!'

'Shall we have another coffee?' Robert rattled his cup on the table. 'You're being silly.'

'Yes, you are quite right, it was silly,' Frank admitted graciously. Robert assumed an air of smug vindication. 'The captain would never have said "Egad".'

And that was how Frank joined me on the next trip.

chapter ten

'Are you listening to me?' I said.

Hairy finished fashioning a pennant from his boarding card and impaled it carefully onto the pirate ship he had constructed out of paper cups.

'Avidly. You were saying about how important it was from the beginning to choose the right area of France for an expedition, about there being the right proportion of interesting hills to easy plains, and how you had to know the country well to be able to turn up in a town in the evening and be certain that there would be a hotel and you were telling me how appropriate it was that you, the great and clever you, were to lead this expedition and how I ought to be eternally grapefruit or something.'

'Well er... that was the gist of it I suppose.' But Hairy had not finished.

'Having heard all the proclamations about the skill needed to choose a cycling route I find myself asking why, last year, you nearly went to Suffolk instead?'

'Shhh! You must not mention Suffolk. France is very sensitive about it.'

'And why you seemed to spend most of last year's trip either looking for hotels or running away from them?'

'That was a bit below the belt. I would draw your attention to the fact that nothing has gone wrong so far.'

'That's nothing to brag about. We haven't got off the ferry yet. Nothing much can go wrong. The Germans stopped laying mines in the Channel in 1945 and icebergs don't get this far south in summer. What do we do if Frank is not waiting for us in Boulogne?'

'He will be. His ferry gets in half an hour before ours.'

'It's not that one there is it?' Hairy pointed at a rusty dredger which was grovelling amongst the sandbanks of the Varne. Hairy is acutely short-sighted and the fact of being accompanied on holiday was a great bonus for him – there would always be somebody there to show him the way. However, on this occasion I suspected that he was probably exploiting his handicap, so I refused to rise to the bait.

'No that's a dredger.'

'And another thing... I don't want to experience any of those weird encounters that you revelled in last time.'

'You can rest assured that all the skills and all the information that I acquired last year will be placed at your entire disposal this year in an effort to make the trip the success it deserves to be.'

'Pompous twit! Do you want another coffee?'

'Oh yes please.'

'Well get me one as well will you? The bar is over there.'

I carried the coffees back to the little niche that we had carved ourselves from the bedrock of day-trippers.

Suddenly, with absolutely no provocation and with the most peremptory of warning chimes, the tannoy said, *'Will the hotel repair man ring two-three please?'*

Hairy paused, his cup at his lips.

'You know, I've always wondered about these tannoy announcements they make on these ferries, it always sounds as if–'

'Oh look, there's a whale!' I pointed out of the window. O.K. It was not the cleverest of remarks but it was the first subterfuge that I could find on the spur of the moment to make him change the subject.

'Daddy! Come and look at the whale. Daddy, Daddy!' The two children behind us began bouncing up and down on the seat and pointing out of the window.

Passengers passing by, stopped and peered through the spray-stained glass. One man wedged himself into the corner and applied the lens of his video camera close to the glass to avoid reflections. People were jostling in the aisle.

'A whale? Where?'

'Out there, look! Can't you see it? By that sunny patch.'

'Now look what you've done,' Hairy unfairly accused me as he looked around with unease.

Flaunting a contrived innocence, I looked placidly out of the window. I started. There was something out there. I had no idea what it was. A dinghy? A buoy? I could not tell but by the time we had docked at Boulogne, half the passengers on board had seen the whale and were busy describing it to the other half.

On the car deck we discovered that our bicycles were unattainable. They had been completely blocked in by diesel-smelling leviathans full of Irish butter and Welsh lamb.

'I thought you said that we would be first off if we put our bikes here?'

'Well, normally we would be.' I wilted under the criticism. 'I didn't think that they would carry freight on a Sunday.'

'You should have asked me. When I despatch a lorryload to be in Italy at nine o'clock on a Monday morning, it is patently obvious to me that the lorry has to start on Sunday at least.'

'Well, you've got inside information.'

'More like common sense.'

We cleared the customs and passport control and stopped in the small car park to check over our machines. Around us milled swarms of shoppers dragging their shopping bags on wheels, and setting their noses keenly in the direction of the old town and the market.

'Where is he then?' Hairy demanded.

I was at a loss. Frank's ferry had arrived. I could see it rusting happily in the berth. Frank knew Boulogne well enough, we had not misunderstood each other in fixing the rendezvous.

'Oi! You two! Over here!'

'He's over there,' I answered superciliously and turned in the direction of the hail.

'Oh my gawd. He's come on a penny farthing!' Hairy exclaimed.

I said nothing, stunned by the sight of Frank's cheery wave and the penny farthing. I somehow could not accept Hairy's assumption. I felt sure that despite Frank's dreadful personality problems which I am too discreet to refer to, he would have mentioned it beforehand had he intended to tour France with us on a penny farthing. It was the kind of detail that, although outwardly trivial in itself, could have ramifications.

We scooted over to him and discovered that he was surrounded by penny farthings, draisiennes, velocipedes and all kinds of antiquated pedal power. This brought the situation happily back into the kind of perspective that I was equipped to deal with, as did the sight of Frank's proper bike, leaning against the railings. It was a cycle club outing.

'Ha, ha. Look at his face!' Hairy laughed to Frank. 'He thought you had come on a penny farthing!'

'I did not!' I lied.

I thought this was a bit thick given that it was Hairy who had levelled the accusation in the first place.

We set off.

The sky was still overcast when I proudly led my crocodile down the chalky track to the little restaurant that I had discovered on a day trip tour in the previous autumn. I had been regaling them on the approach run with tales of juicy trout and creamy *escalope à la Normande* so that by the time we had pulled up outside, our enzymes were buzzing around our stomach linings in a positive frenzy of anticipation.

The tables were already laid out. They sparkled with an impressive display of bright glasses and white table napkins. This was certainly a development since my previous visit. I wondered if it signified an increase in price. The hour had only just turned midday so we had the choice of tables, or rather, we would have done, had we been allowed to sit down.

'*C'est réservé messieurs,*' the lady said.

'What did she say?' Hairy asked.

'It's reserved.'

'Well we'll sit over here then.'

'*C'est aussi réservé, monsieur.*'

'What about this table here?'

'It can't all be reserved.' Hairy grumbled, 'We'll be here all day if we keep trying tables to find out if they are reserved.'

'*C'est tout réservé,*' the lady gave the lie to Hairy's bald assertion with a grandiose sweep of her lace-clad arm.

'Did she say what I think she said?'

'The entire restaurant is reserved.'

'Juicy fresh trout...' Frank said quietly, to nobody in particular.

'We can try down the road,' I suggested.

'Escalope à la Normande...'

'Frank, that's not helping.'

'Must be a wedding or something,' he muttered as we left.

'On a Sunday?' Hairy asked.

'Could be a Jewish wedding,' I said.

'I'm hungry.'

'Don't panic! We'll go further down the valley.'

The next two cafés were closed.

'Whose idea was it to start on a Sunday?'

'Stop whining and go and see if that café over there is open.'

'Only for paraffin.'

'I don't really feel like paraffin at the moment,' Frank admitted lugubriously, 'I had a coffee on the boat.'

Eventually, at ten minutes to two, when we had resigned ourselves to chewing our handlebar grips and sucking puncture patches, we found an impoverished, worm-eaten bistrot where we ate an omelette.

'Cheer up!' I chivvied them as they dawdled back to their bikes, 'I know a great place to stay tonight!'

Perhaps my timing could have been more studied. They looked at each other and I could detect a sort of communion of understanding growing between them like a suspension bridge, leaving me at the bottom of the gorge.

'Is this it? "The Three Pigeons?"' Hairy looked up at the tired signboard swinging over the door. This was the corner where I had nearly fallen off my bike into the ample arms of the patronne after eighty five miles of meandering across northern France looking for a hotel which would not be in Hesdin.

'I thought you didn't speak French.'

'That wasn't French, it was English.'

'Why don't you go in and see if they are open?' Frank intervened.

The blue-tiled walls had not changed, nor had the saucy postcards pinned up at the end of the bar. Only the patronne had changed. I was convinced that it was not the same woman as the previous year. Not that I could recall her face – I am useless at physiognomy – it was her manner which did not fit in. It was not the open armed, welcoming approach. I am not accusing her of being unfriendly, indeed she was professionally quite *correcte* as the French say. She just lacked the sparkle that I had remembered from my previous visit.

Yes she had rooms and we could put the bicycles in the shed in the car park. I told the others.

'I thought you said that you were allowed to put your bike in the banqueting room last time,' Hairy recalled. He had an annoying facility for storing trivial details and then pulling them out for an airing at awkward moments. Frank came to my aid.

'She could hardly offer to put all three bikes in the banqueting room,' he said.

I smiled gratefully at him.

'They must have small banquets in France then,' Hairy observed.

A scuffling noise from the passageway behind the bar precursed the arrival of an animated doormat which skittered about our ankles and snuffled at our shoes. The lady behind the bar wiped her hands on her apron and turned to her companion.

'These messieurs would like rooms for the night and I have allowed them to put their bicycles in the shed in the park,' she explained to the new arrival who was none other than the patronne from last year. She glanced briefly at the book and then looked up at us three. With a broad grin of recognition she leaned across the bar and shook my hand.

'Why, it's *Monsieur l'Anglais!* You came last year didn't you? I see you've brought friends with you as well. Good, good for business.' She shook hands with the other two whom I noticed were just a little impressed. I felt that my standing had gone up a notch. 'That's alright Marie,' she said to her assistant, 'I will deal with this. Three rooms for you? Dinner tonight?'

'Yes please. We thought we would just pop into Montreuil this afternoon to do the sights. What time should we be back for dinner?'

'Eight o'clock sharp. No later or it will all be gone.' She laughed. 'You know where to put your bikes don't you?' She nodded towards the banqueting room.

'Oh yes, I remember.' I looked pointedly at the other two and stalked down the room.

We cycled gently into Montreuil that afternoon and did the sights. Frank made Hairy and I ride along the top of the ramparts so that he could take a really 'atmospheric' photograph. After the fourth attempt, the atmosphere was beginning to become polluted with obscene suggestions as to what he could do with his camera and his 'arty' poses.

I know little about photography but even I could see that Frank's camera was a law unto itself. I remember him once telling me that he had bartered it from a Russian trawler skipper for a pristine copy of Playboy. All the graduations for focus, aperture and speed were inscribed around the lens barrel in symbols which looked like bent hairgrips.

Frank admitted that he could not read Cyrillic script but explained that photography knew no frontiers and that anybody with a practical working knowledge of cameras could use one in any language. Several days later, when he discovered that he had apparently taken forty seven exposures on a twenty four frame film, he was to regret at least not being able to count in Russian.

On the way back to the hotel, Frank suggested that we ought to try the local beer in a bar at the side of the road. We piled up our bikes against a table and went in. I am tee-total but I am not a campaigner. I don't want to stop the world from enjoying itself. I ordered a lemonade.

'What do you want then Hairy?' Frank started off the discussion.

In my innocence, I was expecting a succinct reply such as 'a beer'. Hairy swept his eye over the bottles arranged along the back of the bar and then across the taps.

'Well, I suppose I ought to try a Stella.'

'Oh yes.' Frank was enthusiastic. 'A Stella. Lovely light taste.'

I looked sideways at them across the top of my glass of lemonade. 'Its only beer.'

'I had thought of a Kronenbourg, but I think it might be too gassy for a hot day.'

'Yes. You need something flatter, with a tangy taste to it. A Stella should do nicely.'

I looked from one to the other in disbelief. Were they serious or were they teasing me? I could not discount this latter possibility.

'Do you want it *chambrée* or *frappée*?' I enquired with overt sarcasm.

They thought for a moment.

'I think I would prefer it cold but of course, the room temperature does bring out the full, musty flavour.'

They ordered beers. Tasted them, lauded them and exchanged appreciative observations. They swilled froth around the rim of the glass and pouted at it, they held glasses up to the sunlight and squinted through them. They sipped and savoured. They nodded at each other. The suspension bridge of earlier had strengthened into a communion of beliefs from which I was excluded.

I drank my lemonade and noted the name on the bottle for future reference. It was called 'Sic'.

I lay in my bed that night and wondered why I had not been able to see the moon through the roof in the corridor. Perhaps it was cloudy. No doubt the others would simply catalogue it as another wild and exaggerated traveller's tale but I had seen it last year, I had. Protesting my innocence to the darkened room, I drifted off to sleep.

On the morrow, it was obvious over breakfast that Frank and Hairy had benefited from their night's repose, as they enthusiastically splattered the map, my map, with the crumb and apricot jam proposals for the day's itinerary. I let them run on for a while, one does not like to quash enthusiasm, the secret is to direct it towards its proper goal.

'Actually, I thought that we would go to Abbeville today. It's only about thirty, or thirty five miles but we can take them slowly. Make them last.'

Hairy fixed his face to the print on the map. As I explained yesterday, he is very short sighted.

'Where is Abbeville?' he said.

'Under your left nostril,' Frank remarked and added for good measure, 'By that spot of jam.'

'I've got news for you, that's not jam.'

'Oh, don't be so revolting! Use a handkerchief, not my map.'

''Course if you were a Spitfire pilot you wouldn't have to make this terrible choice, they had their maps printed on their handkerchiefs.'

'Don't encourage him,' I chastised Frank. He really can be quite reckless sometimes.

'No, I was wrong,' Hairy said, licking the tip of his finger. 'It is jam.'

'Give me my map!'

'Just a minute. I haven't finished.'

'Once again, now wipe,' Frank chanted quietly.

'FRANK! Stop it.'

'Sorry.'

'Where are we going to have lunch? I think we ought to know.'

'I second that.'

'We'll buy food in Crécy and picnic in the forest.'

'Sort of egg and Crécy sandwiches?'

'If you like.'

We loaded our bikes outside and then came back in and paid our bill. Madame selected a picture postcard from the rack by the till and handed it to me with my change.

'There you are monsieur. A present. No, no. I give it to you. It is our hotel. Good publicity. A man came over in an aeroplane and took the photo. From the air,' she explained, just in case I had thought that he had taken it from a submarine

'Thank you madame. See you next year!'

'Au revoir.'

'What did she give you?'

'This aerial photo of the hotel.'

'Why?'

'Regular customer. Once a year.' Hairy grunted rudely. 'Hey! Wait a minute you two!' I shouted in excitement, 'Look at this card '

'Well? So what?'

'What do you see?'

'It's a photograph of the hotel from the air. Well, mostly the roof actually.'

'Exactly. The roof. It's a new roof! Look, they are brand new tiles. Last year it was the old half-circular orange tiles. See! That's why you couldn't see the moon and stars through the tiles last night. It's a brand new roof. Photographic proof ye doubting Thomases!'

Hairy looked at Frank. 'It's a bit drastic, hiring a plane just to add credence to your story,'

'We believed you, anyway,' Frank said in a flat voice. 'Honest we did.'

chapter eleven

As we approached Crécy my stomach began to flutter in excitement. You see, I had prepared a little surprise for them. It was not by pure chance that our route had led this way. It was by design. I have always had an itching to be a bit of a tourist guide ever since I stopped being one. Whoops! Now my secret is out. Yes, I admit, once upon a time I was a tourist guide. I used to drag coach loads of goggle-eyed trippers across the decor and tell them tales of wolves and galloping horses and such things.

Back to the present. I had swotted up on the Battle of Crécy before leaving England. I knew how many archers, what time of day, the colour of the pennants and what Edward III had eaten for breakfast. My plan was to explain the unfurling of the battle to them on the actual ground where it took place. It would be a presentation they would never forget but for the moment, it was a secret.

I was searching the left hand side of the road now. I was looking for the tower which I knew had been constructed on the site of the famous windmill from which Edward III had directed the battle.

'Hairy! Frank! Can we just go down here for a minute?' They followed meekly. They were very well behaved really. 'Just put the bikes here, we need to go up that tower.' They did as I bade them.

'Had it occurred to you?' I asked them as we viewed the panorama, 'What Crécy-en-Ponthieu is famous for?'

'Water cress ?'

'Punctures ?'

It can be hard work sometimes, educating the unwilling.

'The Battle of Crécy!' I revealed.

'What, you mean, THE Battle of Crécy? The one in the history books?'

'Yes, that very one.'

'It was here?'

They perused the serene landscape in wonderment and then I launched off. I gave them the works, I spared no effect. 26 August 1346, sun rising over that wood over there, dissipating the mist from this valley but not reaching the gully to our left. Edward III, coming up from Normandy, fighting his way northwards, not southwards into France as you would expect. Phillip VI of France with his horsemen. Edward prepared his lines... Phillip, impulsive, headstrong, rushing straight in... the air, thick with arrows from the English longbows... horses screaming and wheeling... the retreat down that gully to our left... thousands left on the battlefield... hacked down in the wood as they fled... It was inspired. It was majestic. My presentation was faultless.

I stopped, worn out. These battles are such a tiring business. They were both still looking at me. Their initial, polite interest had changed into a mixture of reluctant enthusiasm when they had realised that they could not escape, and concern, lest they could not stop me.

'How many Frogs did we kill?'

Isn't it funny how they always want figures?

'About twenty thousand.'

'That's an awful lot of people to be killed in one day in one place.'

We walked languidly around the top of the tower and then slowly descended. I was spent. It is not every day that you enact the Battle of Crécy single-handed before lunch. Frank wandered over to the notice board and began scratching his upper lip. I would later learn to recognise this signal as a portent.

'There's a chart here of the battle. With coloured arrows and things on it.'

I did not know what to say. Just how insensitive could you be? I had just risked life and limb and probably knocked ten years off my life, reliving the battle of Crécy for them, fighting on both sides, with sound effects and a contemporary political appraisal and he wanted to look at a chart with coloured arrows on it! It reminded me of a brainy schoolfriend I once had who accompanied me to the cinema and brought the book with him to read in case he didn't like the film.

Frank was frowning now and scratching his lip furiously. He looked down the gully on our left. I expect he could still see the writhing bodies and the squealing horses. I do a great squealing horse impression with a little wriggling twist to represent it falling over. Always knocks 'em cold!

'Actually...' Frank began, apologetically as he turned through ninety degrees. 'They came up that gully there.' He pointed away to an insignificant scar to our right, not nearly as impressive as my gully. 'And it wasn't that wood, it was those woods over there.'

'Oh was it? Well you get the general idea. Let's go and buy lunch.'

You have to be thick skinned to be a tourist guide.

As planned, we lunched in the forest. I knew that there would be several picnic areas provided with tables and benches and we made ourselves comfortable on one which was situated plumb in the middle of the *zone de silence*. In deference to the concept, we tried whispering to each other throughout the meal but had to abandon it because we could not hear each other above the noise of the wind hissing through the leaves. They ought to breed a sort of aerodynamically silent tree that could be planted in these *zones de silence*.

To reach the site we had been obliged to ride through a short stretch of woodland, so Hairy and I had plunged impetuously from the road and crackled and crunched our way through the dead twigs and leaves. Then we noticed that Frank was no longer with us. We looked back. He was walking his bicycle down the path.

'Perhaps he's got a puncture' Hairy suggested.

He had not. It was because he considered that his bicycle was much too fragile for the sort of ungentlemanly behaviour that we had just exhibited.

Perhaps this is as good a time as any to get the technical bit over so that you can enjoy the rest of the book, or at least, understand some of it. If there is one thing guaranteed to discourage a reader, it is enthusiastic perorations about backward-bending baffle sprockets and the like, so I will keep my remarks to the general.

Rather as owners come to resemble their pets, so do cyclists reflect the characteristics of their machines. Frank's bike, for example, exuded a lean strength just as Frank did when he was cycling easily alongside us, his struggling companions. Like Frank, it was economical. It did not have much on it. Not much mudguard, not much luggage, not much paint. Frank had pared down his requirements for the journey so that they fitted into one sagging bag. His bicycle was condensed to the fundamental two wheels, handlebars and saddle. This meant that he was unwilling to cycle over rough ground because his wheels and tyres were thinner than ours and less resistant to damage.

Hairy was a complete contrast. His was a real 'belt and

braces' job. Strapped around it were four enormous bags crammed with the vital paraphernalia for the same journey. In his fit of enthusiasm, he had made the mistake of buying large bags and had then felt obliged to fill them. His bicycle was festooned with numerous lights, dynamos, bells, speedometers and water bottles. Clamped to the handlebars was a patent little thingey for holding his map so that it got wet when it rained and he had a nifty attachment to his pannier bags to enable him to dry his washing in the cloud of dust thrown up from the wheels. Had he pulled a shaving brush from his handlebar end and a coffee percolator from the seat pillar, I would not have choked on my peppermint.

True to form, my bicycle was an accurate reflection of my personality. It was naturally modest and perfectly balanced, neither given to vulgar flamboyance nor studied parsimony. I was proud of it and I felt sure that were it ever given the opportunity and the means, it would express its complete contentment with the sensitivity and leadership diplayed by its proprietor.

Despite this sensitivity I should have been more aware of the ramifications of Frank's unwillingness to leave the tarmac. Since the charm of the route that I had sketched out for the expedition was derived largely from 'short cuts' across woods or down farm tracks, it was obviously a route which would prove itself incompatible with the comfort of Frank.

We packed up and I led them off southwards towards Abbeville.

'We're ten miles from Abbeville and its only two o'clock in the afternoon. We'll get there too early,' Hairy observed helpfully.

'No, I had planned it that way,' I lied. 'We can find a hotel, dump our things and then perhaps take a ride out to St.Valéry-sur-Somme.'

'Sounds alright,' Frank concurred.

I thanked him with my eyes.

'Why would we want to go to St.Valéry?' Hairy asked, pinpointing the weakness in my argument. The truthful answer should have been, 'To fill in the time because we are arriving too early at Abbeville because I made a mistake'. The truth is not always practical.

'Don't forget that there is a canal from Abbeville to the sea. I thought we could ride along the towpath and perhaps take a look at the sea lock. I suppose there must be one?' I finished tantalisingly. I knew that Hairy had an insatiable interest in canals.

'Oh well that's alright then. As long as it wasn't just to fill in time because we had arrived too early at Abbeville. That would be too much like time-wasting.'

I quickly distracted him. 'Turn right here!'

'That sign says that Abbeville is straight on,' Frank pointed out.

'Ah yes, but that is by the main road. I want to go down this track here and come into Abbeville by the back door, as it were.' I showed him the map. He raised his eyebrows and said nothing. In the minute, deserted village I found the church and swung down the track at the side. Frank stopped at the entrance and looked at it.

'Are you sure this is the right way?'

I made a show of looking at my map and then at the two white chalk ruts in the grass. I nodded encouragingly,

'Yes this is the one. Come on!'

Hairy and I thundered down the track in a cloud of chalk dust and chippings. It would be downhill for a mile and a half to Abbeville which was just as well for the track would have been too difficult to ascend on a bicycle. Frank tottered on gingerly behind us, picking his route carefully from one tuft of grass to the next but he had to admit that it was peaceful and the gently sloping hills exuded warmth and welcome towards us.

Hairy showed himself to be a bit reckless when let loose in an area of no traffic. Given that he could not see very well and was thus more liable to annihilation from the traffic than we were, he tended to go mad when put in a traffic-free environment. Here, the greater risk of injury came not from others but from your own ability to control the bike. He had pulled quite a distance ahead and was bucking and jumping across the ruts, his bags flopping up and down like the jowls on a bloodhound. Then he stopped. His cloud of white dust drifted slowly past him as he looked back and waited for us to catch up.

'Where do we go now?' he asked smugly.

I could see why. The track led between gateposts into an expanse of rough, downland meadow through which there was no discernible trace of a road, track or path. I pulled out the map and looked at the sun like they do on the films.

'It's still up there,' Hairy said. 'You can tell by the heat on the back of your neck and the fact that we haven't put our lights on yet.'

'What's the problem?' Frank asked cautiously as he skittered up, his back wheel slipping sideways down the edge of a rut in a minor avalanche of chalk.

'No problem!' I said with more gaiety and conviction than I felt. We would have to go on into the unknown. It would be inciting mutiny to suggest that we try to cycle back up the route we had just descended. 'The track goes on down there around the hill.'

'If you say so.' Hairy fearlessly launched himself out into the meadow.

Frank drew his breath in a long sibilance and then dismounted and began to walk his bike down the edge of the field, I tucked my map into the pocket on my pannier bag and, grabbing both handlebars firmly, began to coax my bike over the hussocks and tussocks. We talked in a desultory fashion, Frank lithely wheeling his light bike over the grass and me thumping and lurching alongside him. We politely discussed the merits and demerits of walking as compared to cycling and debated upon the position of the intangible line on one side of which it was easier to cycle and on the other side of which it would be more sensible to walk. We agreed amicably that each person should have his own interpretation of where the line lay and that others in the group should respect this whilst all members should strive to do everything to ensure that individual interpretations did not tear the fabric of the communal whole to ruin.

I felt, modestly, that this little discussion with Frank had helped him to cope with any stirrings of guilt that he might have felt at having put us all out by selfishly insisting on walking when it was patently obvious to the most timid of maiden aunts that the field was a perfectly safe cycling environment.

Hairy was waiting for us at the end of the spur. He pointed to two gateways about a hundred yards distant, from which two chalky tracks led in diverging directions.

'Gotta be one of those.'

'Hang on, I'll look at the map.'

'You'll need binoculars if you want to look at it from here,' Frank remarked. 'It fell out of your bag at the top of the field. Look, you can just see it. That patch of white by the clump of thistles.'

'Why didn't you tell me?'

'Well we were having such an interesting discussion. Anyway, you could do with a walk.' He grinned, 'Cos you'll never be able to cycle back up there.'

He was right.

chapter twelve

We dropped down into Abbeville by the track which ran level and then suddenly plunged over the escarpment like a waterfall. Throwing caution to the winds, we hurtled down it, whooping and yelling like children and then self-consciously pedalling quietly on the flat, regaining our breath and trying to ignore each other's faces which were flushed with excitement.

By half past three we were discussing hotels, standing on the truncated avenue which led to the railway station. The choice was either a smart, neat hotel-restaurant or a large dilapidated Hotel de la Gare. I preferred the latter but as it transpired, the choice was made for us.

In the neat hotel, a perfectly obnoxious man, whom I suspected of being Dutch, when we enquired of him if he had rooms, asked us immediately if we intended dining there. We had not noticed the restaurant, we had not inspected the menu. For all we knew it could have been a perfect bijou of a restaurant but as far as we were concerned from that moment on, nothing would entice us to eat there. If the vacancy of the rooms depended upon the patronage of the restaurant then we could only suspect that it was either too dear or that there was a better restaurant opposite.

When we vacillated and tentatively suggested that we might go and see some hastily invented friends in St. Valéry, he rudely expressed his preference for us to eat with our friends and stay with our friends and not bother him.

I wanted to be as rude to him as he had been to us but as we left I could think of nothing more insulting than, 'I suppose you are Dutch.'

Once outside we jointly and vehemently wished a pestilence upon his head. May his cook run off with his wife and the barman abscond with the till. Don't laugh! Next time I went through Abbeville the hotel had closed down and was boarded up. You don't mess with cyclists!

Whilst Hairy did something unspecified to his bicycle in the hotel yard, probably re-calibrating his radar or something, Frank and I discussed rooms with the patronne of the Hotel de la Gare. Much to her amusement, we kept the baths to ourselves and allotted Hairy the room *sans bain.* We explained to her that if she didn't tell him, then neither would we and if kept in ignorance he would be quite happy. This quasi-Stalinistic approach to hotel room allocation functioned admirably and I suspect that it was adopted tacitly thereafter whenever one member was not present at the negotiations. After a quick wash and brush up, we reassembled downstairs in the bar.

It was still a sunny afternoon outside and I could see that if I didn't do something soon, then I would spend the hours before dinner propped up at the zinc, watching Hairy and Frank pour French beer down their throats and making pretentious observations about 'flavour' and 'body'. This genus of commentary which borders on the fatuous when applied to wine becomes downright ludicrous when appended to beer. I resurrected my suggestion of a trip out to St. Valéry and was astonished at the alacrity with which they accepted it. It transpired that the thought of seeing me pulling a long face whilst they imbibed would quite spoil their enjoyment.

We verified with the patronne that dinner was at 19.30 and were amused at her incredulity upon learning that we intended to make a thirty kilometre trip on bicycles before dinner, just for fun. We left her sadly clucking and shaking her head as only non-cyclists do.

As you know, my original intention had been to cycle there and back along the towpath but after a mile or two of bone-jarring, palm-numbing pedalling into a buffeting breeze which blew off the sea and roared in our ears, we unanimously decided that the smooth tarmac of the undulating *départementale* was preferable.

We found the lock and Hairy expressed himself satisfied with it after an inspection of the secrets of its function. I, however, had found something else to puzzle over. Laid in the bed of the swing bridge was a railway track but it appeared strange.

'Is it an optical illusion produced by the absence of sleepers or is that track narrower than usual?' I asked.

We measured the gap with our feet and came to the conclusion that it was a metre gauge.

'I didn't know that there were any metre gauge lines still being used in this part of France,' I said to myself.

'Maybe it isn't.'

'The tracks are shiny.'

'Could be caused by cars running across them.'

I followed the tracks with my eye to where they left the road and burrowed under some heavy foliage. I could still see a glint of light.

'They are still shiny over there and cars don't drive up there.'

We walked over to the leafy corridor and suddenly came across a rake of bizarre old carriages. They were wooden and sported open platforms at each end. It was now obvious from the state of the track and the repair of the carriages that this line was used as a tourist attraction at certain times of the year.

'Well I'm blowed,' Frank said.

But the sight of those old carriages stirred an obscure memory in some distant cul de sac of my brain. As fantastic as it could be, I knew that I had seen these coaches before. I had seen them... I closed my eyes. I had seen them... unrepaired, lying in a siding, with their quaint locomotives. I thought hard. I had seen them through a railway carriage window, streaked with grey winter rain. It must have been many years earlier when I used to travel to Paris and back by train every week. That was it. I had seen these coaches before they had been saved. I knew it.

'What are you doing?'

'I just need to look at the map,' I replied.

'We know where we are.'

'For once,' Frank added.

'It's not that. It's something else.' I traced the line on the map with my finger and experienced a bizarre thrill when I discovered that it ran into a station which connected with the main line from Paris to Calais.

'Happy now?'

'Yes. I just wanted to check something.' I could not explain. They would not have been interested, nor would they have understood.

We climbed to the top of the town and stood looking over the wall at the broad, muddy, brown estuary of the River Somme. Far across the bay winked the town with the singularly unappetising name of Le Crotoy. The steady breeze tugged at our hair and whipped up the white crests of the advancing sea which was still far out in the bay.

Hairy cleared his throat and even before he had begun

to speak, I could hear the thunder of galloping hooves.

'You know...' he surveyed the flat waste of ooze, spread before us like a vast brown blancmange and lightly rippled by a trickle of the Somme, 'I bet this is one of those places where the tide comes in faster than a–'

'There's a bar over there,' I interrupted him. They both seemed surprised at this. Not so much at the location of the bar, but rather that I should have drawn their attention to it.

It was long and narrow like a verandah and from it we could watch the gulls paddling and poking their bills into the slime.

'What'll you have then, Frank? A Kronenbourg?'

'A bit too heavy.' Frank pondered. 'I've a mind to try that Killian's.'

'If you want something lighter, you'd be better off with a Jupiler.'

[Editor's note: No, this is not a spelling mistake. The name of the beer is indeed JUPILER. *You have misread it as* JUPITER *on French café awnings all your life. Look carefully at it next time.]*

Frank rubbed his chin whilst his eyes scanned along the shelves of bottled beers. The bar lady stood back, patiently admiring the connoisseurs in their deliberations. It was obviously most satisfying for her to be able to serve such discerning customers.

'I suppose I could try a Lowenbrau...'

They eventually decided upon a happy choice and secured for themselves tall glasses of frothy beer. I looked at them with distaste as I imagined the volumes of gas contained within each glass and piously comforted myself with being a teetotaller. But was I going to have to put up with this performance every time they wanted a drink? I would have to do something about it.

'And for you?' the barlady enquired.

'A glass of water please. Bottled water,' I added and glowered at the other two.

She plunged her hand below the bar and pulled out a bottle of Vittel shaped like a juggler's club. She handled it much as a juggler would have done.

'Have you got Badoit?' I enquired sweetly.

'Pardon?' She paused in mid-movement.

'Have you got Badoit water? It is my favourite.'

She looked at me for a second and then, deciding that I was serious, replaced the bottle and searched below the bar.

'No Badoit, but I've got Contrexeville.' She evidently laboured under the impression that I needed the water for medicinal purposes and not just because I liked drinking it.

'Oh not Contrexeville!' I turned up my nose. 'Don't you find those waters from the Vosges have got just too much magnesium in them? Have you got an *eau pétillante?*'

Hairy coughed into his froth and glanced at Frank. She disappeared below the bar again.

'Perrier?' she proffered. At least she had the grace to inflect her voice to convey her lack of conviction.

'Too gassy and too much salt.'

Both beer glasses now stood unattended on the bar.

'I've got a Vichy,' she suggested in desperation.

'Aah! Now I like a nice Vichy...' She straightened up with a smile of relief and Frank and Hairy sighed and made a grab for their beers. '...provided it is the right Vichy.'

'The right Vichy? But it's only water!' Hairy imitated my critique of yesterday.

'Tell me, is it Vichy Célestins or Vichy St. Yorre? They are different sources. Quite different.'

'I... I... don't know,' she admitted.

'Show me the label.' She held up a bottle to me. 'That's St. Yorre. I prefer the Vichy Célestins. You had better just give me a glass of Vittel.'

'Gladly!' She poured out a glassful on the bar. Frank and Hairy were struck dumb, their beer going flatter by the second, their mouths, sagging open.

'Cheers!' I turned, raised my tumbler and, nodding at

their inert glasses, I asked innocently, ''Beer all right?'

Before we left St. Valéry we cast an eye over the monument to commemorate the departure of William the Conqueror for England in 1066. Then we swooped silently down through the almost deserted pedestrian street. Well, not quite silently, for as we passed by two ladies who, with their arms full of loaves, were chatting outside the boulangerie, the first effects of the Kronenbourg made themselves obvious as, with a sound like ripping sailcloth, Frank flatulated. Pigeons took to the wing in alarm and the two women burst out laughing. Perhaps one day they will have a monument to Frank's digestion.

Frank and Hairy, perhaps wisely, said nothing about my performance in the bar but presumably decided to expunge the memory, for, after dinner, whilst I prudently retired to bed, they recklessly decided to stay up late in the bar and drink lots of beer. When they were well pickled at about half past one in the morning, a man came in carrying a dustbin which he put down at the side of them before ordering a beer. They looked into it. It was writhing full of live eels. They decided to go to bed.

鞠躬盡瘁

FAITHFUL unto DEATH

Nº 48954
Li Shih Kuei
Chinese Labour Corps
Died April 28ᵀᴴ 1919

chapter thirteen

I cannot really say much about the following morning.
We cycled gently up the valley of the Somme towards the
restaurant where Monsieur Richard had fascinated me
with his reminiscences of the early days of flying. My
companions seemed peculiarly jaded. They did not speak
much and when they did, it was to recount the episode
concerning the eels. They had expected some sympathy
from me and so they were consequently mortally offended
when I burst out laughing and opined that it served them
right. They exchanged a look of suffering between them
that would have qualified them for professional affiliation
to the Martyrs' Union. It had still not occurred to me
that they were quite simply experiencing what, I believe, is
called a hangover.

To make matters worse, we drank our morning coffee in
a dirty little hovel of a bar and Hairy left his potty behind
and did not realise this until he had cycled half a mile and
then had to go back to fetch it. Perhaps in fairness to Hairy
and to ward off all inferences of micturition or enuresis, I
should explain that his 'potty' was his plastic crash helmet

which he very sensibly wears when cycling. He does not call it his potty, of course, and he doesn't like us to, but you know what friends are.

Lunch was good but old Monsieur Richard was not there. I wondered what had happened to him but dared not ask because I was frightened that they might tell me. Somehow our conversation of last year was made more precious by his absence this year.

Outside the restaurant, we discovered that Hairy had secured for himself a puncture in the rear tyre, the most difficult, naturally. Inverting his bicycle was not a simple operation, involving as it did, the unstrapping and removal of his four pannier bags, taking off his two water bottles so that they did not drip water down your neck and generally ensuring that all the other accessories which sprouted from the framework did not bend, break, go out of adjustment or reprogram themselves.

Once we had removed the tyre, it became apparent that today's puncture was merely a repeat performance of yesterday's. I had not bothered you with the trivia, but on the previous day, on entering the outskirts of Abbeville, Hairy had got a puncture in this very tyre. When we had stopped to repair it, a man had come scurrying across the road from his house, carrying a sheet of sandpaper to roughen up the inner tube, as you must. The paper was so coarse it could have come out of an elephant's manicure set. Had we used it, it would have shredded the inner tube and left it looking like a box of liquorice allsorts. However, all this is peripheral. What was important was that we had been unable to find the object in the tyre which had caused the puncture. Finding it is essential since if it is not removed, it simply punctures the new inner tube when it is pumped up. And this is what had happened. By the size and location of the hole it appeared probable that it had been caused by the same object as yesterday.

Frank edged his fingers around the inside of the tread, kneading it expertly.

'Got it!' he suddenly exclaimed.

It was a minute sliver of glass, embedded firmly in the rubber so that once the tube was at full inflation, it only required the wheel to drop over a hefty bump for it to pierce the tube. I held the tyre splayed out and with the delicacy of an eye surgeon, Frank winkled out the glass with the end of a small screwdriver.

We reassembled the bike, popped the bottles back into place, restrapped the bags on the racks, pulled all the levers and consulted all the dials and pronounced it to be one hundred per cent fit. Just before we pulled away, I asked Frank,

'What did you do with the bit of glass?'

'Oh I threw it down on the ground somewhere.'

'That was pretty clever. It's probably back in the tyre again by now!'

'Yes, that was a bit stupid.'

I nearly fell from my machine in astonishment to hear such an admission from Frank. Perhaps all those terrible personality disorders that I am much too kind to mention become mollified on a cycle ride.

But Frank had not exhausted his supply of surprises for the day. As we cycled up the valley, wondering at the strange mixture of red brick working-man's terraced cottages separated by huge tracts of arable land, a cyclist overtook us. Up until then, all of the cyclists that we had seen, and they had been surprisingly few, had greeted us in some way or another. Possibly they greeted us not as cyclists but merely as travellers using the same road.

From our observations we had concluded that the French do not go cycle-touring. They use bicycles to go to and from work, to get the shopping or to go to school. On Sundays they all pile onto their stripped down racers and sweat around the lanes, timing each other on a circuit or pacing a rider for twenty kilometres. From the French point of view, what we had done was to take our work bikes, strap all manner of encumbrances upon them and then set off into the void. This was a concept that they could not cope with and so this is why I say that they greeted us not as cyclists, for it was not apparent to them what we were really doing.

The chap who pedalled past us must have been a Sunday rider who had got lost. His racing bike sparkled with stainless steel spokes and chromium front forks, the thin racing tyres hissed over the tarmac as he swished past us and the yellow and magenta of his cycling jersey reflected garishly in our sunglasses. When compared to the three lumbering juggernauts that he had just overhauled, he assumed the dimensions and the qualities of the sleekest of sports cars which was why it was so incongruously funny when I clicked my fingers, pointed at his disappearing blur and ordered,

'After him Frank!'

How we laughed! Then Frank was off, standing up on his pedals, his machine lurching from side to side. We still thought that he was joking.

'Ataboy Frank!'

Having achieved the initial acceleration to take him up a gear, he sat, his legs pounding powerfully on the pedals.

'My god, he's going to catch him!'

We had to pedal faster to keep the duo in sight on the winding road. It was utterly ridiculous for a rider on a loaded touring bicycle to try to catch a racer. We thundered around the corner to see that Frank was only a cycle length from the racer's back wheel. Too late his quarry looked around and realised that he was being pursued.

Frank tore past as we cheered wildly from fifty yards behind. Whether it was this cheering or the sight of Frank's royal blue bottom on a rusty orange bicycle that unnerved the rider we shall never know but, possibly in a last minute attempt to retain some credibility, he veered off down a farm track to make it appear that he had arrived at his destination.

We swooped up to Frank, slapped him heartily on the back and relived the whole stupid exploit, chattering excitedly, trying to imagine what the racer had felt when overtaken by a tourer who had already travelled thirty miles that day and eaten a heavy lunch.

'He's probably slashing his wrists right now.' Hairy suggested melodramatically.

It was certainly not an achievement that the rider would rush to recount to his club colleagues. Unwittingly, by his whimsical adoption of a facetious proposal, Frank had introduced into our cycling holiday what was to become a tradition, all the more valued, for its never being abused.

The afternoon's tourist exploit was to be a visit of the caves in the region. I like to add a little culture to what you must be thinking was merely one long binge of drinking and depravity. When we arrived at the car park, however, three coaches were parked in the baking heat. I ran a professional eye over them.

'One hundred and fifty Parisian school children,' I said. 'From a working class district of Paris.'

'I am not all that bothered about caves,' Frank said.

'And it will probably be cold inside,' Hairy added for good measure.

'That's settled then. This way!'

I don't always lead the threesome. At some stage everybody wants to go in front. I always make sure that I am in a position to direct when we come to a difficult crossroads but otherwise I am quite happy to play 'French Generals' and lead from the rear. It was after the caves, as we strung ourselves out over a long straight climb that Hairy, who was second in line, sniffed and shouted forward to Frank.

'Is that you?'

'Is what me?'

I wrinkled my nose at the distasteful odour.

'I see what you mean. Is it you, Frank?'

'Pooh! It's turning my stomach.'

Frank dropped back alongside us.

'If you want to go at the front, you can,' he remarked.

Mindful of the responsibility of the expedition leader to keep things together even at great personal sacrifice, I assumed the mantle of front rider. Frank and Hairy continued to talk behind my back.

'You'd think he would at least say pardon.'

'I think it's worse now that he is leading.'

'Funny, he had the same to eat as we did. What does he do with it?'

'I don't know but I wish he would stop it.'

The accusations and counter accusations continued around the triangle, nobody would admit proprietorship of the odour. By the time that we had reached the summit of the incline we were three warring factions, forming alliances and breaking them as easily. So engrossed were we in this conflict, that we cycled past the yellow lorry which was crawling down the other side of the hill, without affording it the slightest attention. It was only when we noticed that the odour had magically dissipated, that we stopped and looked back to discover that the lorry was spraying herbicide on the grass verge.

Mind you, I still think it was Frank.

The afternoon sort of fell apart after that. We straggled along the top of the lumpy northern valley wall of the Somme. Frank forged on ahead of us so that at one point I had difficulty in making him hear directions and we had to go the way that he was pointing rather than the way that I had chosen on the map. This annoyed me and I feared I might have shown it in the caustic observations that I made about 'cycling together' and 'helping each other' but I had no need to worry for Frank was utterly impervious to my lancinating recriminations.

I should also admit that the road was not the prettiest route that we had found thus far but I received their terse comments like blows to the body.

'Another bloody dumper truck.'

'Look out, pot holes.'

'Mind this cement dust blowing across the road.'

'Oh goody, what a pretty chemical factory.'

I felt like shouting that my map did not show dumper trucks or pot holes or cement dust and that if they felt that they could do any better then they could damn well do it themselves but I held my tongue. When I became more experienced and less sensitive I realised that my map could show me things like dumper trucks and cement dust if I bothered to read it intelligently, but for the present, I just felt oppressed.

To cap it all, when we reached Amiens which was to be our stop for the night, I got unashamedly lost. I had confidently announced that there were thousands of hotels dotted around the station and that nobody could miss the station in Amiens. I led them off around deserted streets, following the signs to the *'Gare S.N.C.F. St. Roch'* until I lost the signs and my bearings and my confidence all in one go. How conceited could I be to think that I could lead them faithfully to the railway station on the knowledge gained after one overnight visit a year ago!

I had to admit that I did not recognise this area of Amiens at all and that I needed to consult the map. They patiently waited for me to decide where we were and where we should go. They did not tease me nor did they criticise. They are not a bad couple of companions really.

I discovered my foolish mistake and was almost too embarrassed to admit to it. Amiens has two railway stations and I was aiming at the wrong one. The station that I had known, was situated in the extreme south east of Amiens and was called, inappropriately, the '*Gare du Nord*'. I should have been prepared for this twisted logic for I was familiar with Canterbury West station which can be found due north of Canterbury East station. It would appear that railway companies throughout Europe use their own version of the compass.

Later than I had hoped, we stopped at the small hotel that I had stayed at last year, the one with the crushed glass yard. At first the lady opened the register willingly and assured me that she had a room for me but when the other two ambled in she appeared uncertain.

'I have only got one room left,' she apologised. 'A single room.' Her husband did a toe-drag shuffle in his slippers up to the counter and inspected the register. He nodded confirmation.

'Yes, we only have one bed, messieurs.'

'What shall we do?' I asked the others.

'I think we should stick together.'

'So do I. Ask them if they know of another hotel.'

'Better still, get them to phone and book us at another hotel.'

The old couple scratched their heads and then she said to him,

'Al*ors, Chez Zidi là...*' An expression of horror and doubt flashed across the old man's face but the woman justified her choice with a scathing, '*Mais ils ne risquent rien voyons, ce sont des hommes pas des nanas!*'

'Well that's settled then,' I announced brightly to the others. 'I know where she means, it is just around the corner.'

We thanked them and walked out to our bicycles. I thought I had got away with it but I had forgotten that Frank could speak French.

'What did she say to her hubby? I didn't quite catch it.' he said.

'Oh, I don't know, I wasn't listening.' I said, but my stomach was turning somersaults of misgiving as I led them through the back streets of Amiens with the lady's words ringing in my ears.

'They'll be in no danger, will they? They are men, not bits of skirt!'

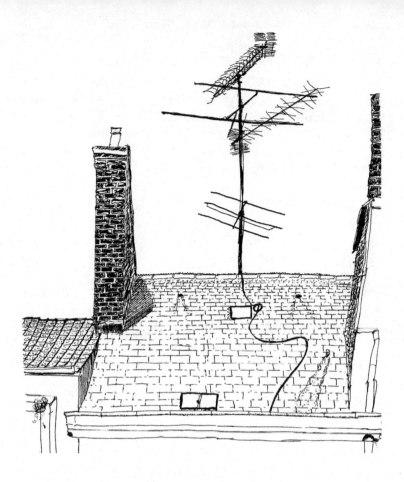

chapter fourteen

'Did you sleep all right?' Hairy enquired.

'Apart from your snoring,' Frank grumbled.

'I didn't realise that we had to go three to a room.'

'Sounded like thirty three.'

I snapped a piece of rubbery bread from the stick and as I buttered it, wondered if I ought to tell them or whether they would get there on their own. I decided to say nothing and wait.

'Unusual sort of hotel, isn't it?'

'How d'ya mean? Pass the coffee.'

'It's all upstairs. We came in the front door, paid at that cubby hole with the till and went straight up to the rooms.

'Yes... there aren't any facilities are there? You would expect a lounge or a table with magazines or something.'

'And why did we have to pay first? Never had to do that that before. This bread's lousy isn't it?'

'And we had to pay ten francs per bike to park them under the stairs. I thought that was a bit cheeky. Look out, here comes Abdul!'

The discussion stopped whilst the man who was presumably 'Zidi' himself, since we had seen nobody else, carried a milk jug into the room.

'Everything all right messieurs?'

We switched on bright smiles and assured him of our absolute contentment. The door closed behind him. Hairy continued.

'And is he the only one running this hotel?'

'How do we know it is a hotel? Did you see a name over the door?'

'There was a neon sign. It said *hotel*.'

'Hotel what?'

'Just *hotel*.'

I still said nothing.

'Take this room for instance. It doesn't really look like a breakfast room does it?'

'Well it's got tables and chairs in it.'

'But it's a bar.'

'That's quite common in France. You often have your breakfast in the bar.'

'I dunno... it seems more like a...' I held my breath as I waited for Frank to continue. '...well I don't know what really. The decorations are a bit flouncy for a French bar.'

'You mean you can't envisage a man coming in here carrying a dustbin full of live eels?'

'He'd never get them up the stairs for a start.'

Now they were wandering right off the point. How frustrating!

'It must be quite a popular hotel though. I could hear people coming and going all through the night. This sugar is like concrete.'

'I couldn't hear anything above the sound of your snoring.'

'Well the hotel must be full if we had to share a room.'

'I suppose you're right. What's in this jam?'

'Oh it's jam is it? I was waiting for you to start it. I didn't know what it was.'

'Just a minute... If this hotel is full, why are we the only people having breakfast?'

'I expect the others know what the breakfast is like.'

'Perhaps they've all left early. Travelling reps. and the like. They usually go out at about seven.'

'Strange though.'

'Very queer.'

We stamped noisily down the bare concrete steps and unravelled our bicycles from their protected parking under the stairs. Outside, the morning was pale blue and fresh and Amiens was rumbling and hooting through its rush hour. There is something entrancing about travelling in a rush hour without being part of the rush. Not needing to be anywhere in particular at a certain time. But we didn't go far. Just around the corner I pulled in and stopped outside a terrace café.

'Come along you two,' I ordered. 'Breakfast. Proper breakfast.'

They looked at each other, shrugged and followed me into the bar.

'Three big black coffees and three *croissants aux beurre.*'

The barman repeated my order and spun around to wrench handles and levers on the espresso machine.

'What is all this in aid of?' Hairy asked.

'My treat. You deserve it.'

They looked at each other again, perplexed.

'Why?'

'Reward for your shining and endearing innocence.'

'What are you on about?'

'You two. It's not every night you sleep in a French brothel is it?'

I regretted not having prepared my camera.

As they weaved in and out of the stationary traffic behind me they indignantly fired questions at me but I could not hear a word of what they said so they had to stew in their own conclusions till we reached the canal.

'Come on. Down here. Let's get away from all this traffic and noise.' I turned off down my secret path through the *hortillonnages*. It wound between the sleeves of silent slack water and the allotments; over plank bridges and past moored punts. After a few hundred yards I knew something was wrong and so I shouted a warning to Hairy that I was stopping. This was to avoid him ramming my back wheel.

'What's wrong?' he said as he rammed into my back wheel. Two hundred yards back, Frank was coaxing his bicycle along the path, walking beside it as if leading a cherished donkey to Nazareth.

'Do you reckon he's got a puncture?'

'No, it's the same as yesterday. The track is too bumpy for him.' I was disgusted. 'I thought we had cured it. This is quickly becoming Frank's Bicycle Walking Tour of France.'

In the morning sun we crept through Corbie and up the sinuous and green valley of the Ancre. At Albert we stopped in the café opposite the Basilica and drank hot chocolate. It was a peculiar choice for a sunny day.

'Funny name for a town – Albert.'

'Well now, it is interesting that you should mention that because it actually got its name from a chap called Albert.

'You don't say,' Hairy observed rudely.

Frank gazed as if in supplication at the cross on the top

of the Basilica.

'I can sense a bit of his tour guide coming out,' he said. 'Go on then. Who was Albert?'

'He was a mate of Louis XIII. The King gave him the town as a present in sixteen hundred and something.'

'And so they named the town after him?'

'Well, not exactly, because his name was Charles.'

'You said it was Albert.'

'It was Charles d'Albert.'

'So Albert was his surname then?'

I could not understand the difficulty they were having with this explanation.

'Yes, I suppose so.'

'Jolly good job his surname wasn't something like Blenkinsop,' Hairy said.

'Or Manchester,' Frank added. 'Where are we going to stop tonight?'

'Bapaume.'

He looked at his watch.

'But we'll be there at about half past two.'

In an unkindly manner I retorted, 'Not if you keep walking we won't.'

It was a silly remark to make and, powerless to stop them, I watched the words leave my mouth in slow motion and then impact home on Frank. He blinked. I regretted the comment but did not appreciate just how much until we left Albert and with a curt, 'Which way now?' Frank took the lead.

He set a cracking pace, oblivious to our feeble protests. With great finesse he demonstrated to us that his type of bicycle might not relish trudging across ploughed fields or abseiling down mine shafts but when it came to riding on the road, a task for which it was designed, his machine was a nonesuch.

Through gritted teeth we laboured on as the gap widened between us. Too proud to call out, we puffed and cursed at the ridiculous weight of our belongings. Hairy in particular must have been reappraising his philosophy of cycle touring and I was certain that if he ever did it again he would do it with a lot less in his bags.

Frank's single, half-empty pannier bag mocked us with a floppy wave each time he skimmed a bump. 'Look how light I am,' it was saying. 'I jump up and down like a fairy whereas your bags crash back into place like piledrivers.'

Soon Frank was so far ahead that he could not hear my directions and we just had to follow him to keep him in sight.

'He must stop soon.' I assured Hairy. 'We're coming to a crossroads. He must stop.'

He did not. He turned to the right as I would have directed him and sped off towards Bapaume.

'I'm stopping,' I declared but Hairy would not have heard me for he was now far behind me.

'Which way did he go?' he asked when he caught up with me.

'That way.'

'Is it the right way?'

'Yes, but I am going to wait until he comes back to look for us.'

'What if he doesn't?'

I made a poor attempt to sound confident. 'He will.'

We waited. To pass the time I tried to think of a famous expression to represent the state of ultimate desperation. Then I just tried to recall any celebrated utterance. I wondered, do people know when they are articulating something which is destined to be inscribed on the tablet of history for all to use? If they do, it rather puts into question the ingenuousness of their opinion. Not many people would want to be remembered for one of their multifarious views taken at random. If they had to leave a monument they would surely prefer to choose the one they considered to be their best.

I suppose this is the nub of the matter. Most of the expressions which pass into normal everyday language are not chosen or promoted, they are merely adopted because they fulfil a need or fit the specification required for the opinion. And how many of those sayings really betray the identity of their author?

There is no doubt in my mind that inventing well known expressions is an ironically unrecognised pastime. It is not the way to become famous. Whenever a phrase becomes popular, some insignificant person vainly and shrilly tries to draw the attention of a deaf-eared world to his claim to having originated it. But it does him no good. He cannot patent it. There are no royalties on it, so why does he bother? The hankering after fame and recognition is doomed to disappointment. The world does not remember the perpetrators, only their perpetrations.

I can talk with some authority on this subject since I had an expression stolen from me. It happened like this. Back in my distant past I was obliged to cross the English Channel regularly by hovercraft. On one of these crossings, a passenger survey was being conducted and I was given a form to fill in. It was quite a simple tick-the-box type reply except for one square which was dedicated to free expression. I was asked how I would best describe the sensation of travelling in a hovercraft.

I was young and impressionable and I rather fancied the hostess in her red hat so I wrote something to the effect that it was like being dragged over a particularly uneven section of Belgian pavé whilst seated in a wooden orange box. It was not necessarily true you understand, but I felt that I had to rise to the challenge and those red hats were rather fetching.

Well, time and the hostess passed me by without a murmur until some five or six years later I found myself in an occupation which impinged upon hovercraft operation. A colleague in the office finding an article about hovercraft in a Sunday colour supplement, read out aloud for the interest of all around.

'Hey listen to this everyone. Riding in a hovercraft has been described as similar to being dragged over bad Belgian pavé whilst seated in a wooden orange box.'

I leaped out of my chair.

'I said that! That was me! I was the first one! I made up that expression. I wrote it down. They copied it. It was me that said it....' And so forth. You can imagine the response from my colleagues. It was exactly the same as mine would have been in their place. Oh the tragedy!

And so, at that French crossroads, symbolic perhaps of the crossroads of life, I invented an expression which, rather than have you steal from me, I offer to you, free from any encumbrance of any sort; for you to use to describe that situation of extreme desperation in which you find yourself when you have considered and rejected all else.

'I was down to the cardboard on the roll.'

Think about it.

Having made his point, Frank came back and we cycled into Bapaume. I was still smarting from their caustic comments on my previous attempt to educate them so I said nothing about the statue celebrating the success of the French general Faidherbe when he pushed the German army back to the Somme. Bapaume, of course, is slap bang in the middle of the battlefields of the Great War. But this was different, for the statue commemmorated a battle in the Franco Prussian War of 1871.

We found a hotel which had the promise of a good restaurant appended to it.

'What do we do now?'

'I've got to deliver some tea.'

'Tea?'

'Tea.'

'You mean TEA tea?'

'Tea tea.'

'O.K.'

'T.T.O.K.?' Hairy questioned, having come in at the end of the brief exchange.

'Do you know the Canal du Nord?' I waved the bait beneath his nose.

'I know of it.'

'To get to my friends' house—'

'To deliver the tea.'

'Correct. We have to cycle past the entrance to the Ruyaulcourt Tunnel.'

We spread the map out on the bar top and Hairy began sniffing his way across it like a bloodhound.

'Can't we go here?' he asked. It was another tunnel, ten miles further east. 'They have overhead electric wires in the tunnel and they tow the boats through with electric tugs. I've read about it. I'd like to see that.'

Frank said, 'So would I.'

They looked at me as though I ought to make a decision. I did. I made the wrong one. I should have checked the direction of the wind. We had come to Bapaume in good time. Another forty miles would be no problem. With a gross of PG Tips tea bags ostentatiously strapped upon my rear pannier, I led them off through the lanes towards the canal and the farm where my friends lived.

Christian was a man of the soil. He smelled of damp, earthy furrows. His face was brown, his head was round and he had begun to look like the mangelwurzels that he cultivated. Nicole, his wife, although of the village, had a certain sophistication about her. She had studied and was now a teacher. It was in this guise that she had come to us with her daughter as a paying guest for two weeks to improve her English. At the end of the two weeks, she had persuaded Christian to come over on the ferry and collect them. That may not sound like an achievement by our standards but he rarely left his *département* and this journey to Calais, albeit at thirty six years of age, was the first time in his life that he had been in a train. It was a stupendous revelation to me that people such as they, existed.

Frank, Hairy and I sat in the neat kitchen, three clumping great blokes, whilst Nicole made us all a pot of tea. People from their farming community began to just 'pop in'. At first, a spurious reason for their detour was proffered but as the word spread around the village that Nicole was entertaining three English cyclists who had delivered her tea direct from England, the subterfuges went by the wayside and plain, honest curiosity was flaunted instead.

Although I would have liked to have welcomed the latter approach as being more worthy, the former at least allowed us a little opportunity for self-deception. We could pretend that we really did believe that cousin Pierre had forgotten his bag of endives and both camps could partake of the manoeuvres which to us, were of a comforting familiarity. But for straightforward nosiness, with all the direct questions and staring that such an attitude involves, we found ourselves to be poorly prepared. And yet it was pure, untainted by social postures and frank. It was a sad indictment of contemporary society that we felt more at home with deceit than truth.

'Feel like a bloody goldfish,' Hairy muttered.

With a sad premonition as to the future of our frail relationship, I said goodbye to Nicole and Christian. To the unspoken but patent relief of my two companions we were soon speeding with the treacherous wind towards the furthest point east that we would attain on this journey.

Frank and I tried to enthuse over the sight of tram wires disappearing into a tunnel full of solid green canal water but any effusiveness upon our part paled besides Hairy's exuberance. It was all that we could do to dissuade him from pedalling off into the darkness.

And then it was time to turn back towards the hotel at Bapaume. Wham! The wind hit us full in the chest. It had obligingly blown us from Bapaume and was now, just as persuasively, trying to convince us to continue on to Vienna.

We slogged it out, heads down, across the rumpled plain of the Artois. We should have taken turns at leading whilst the other two sheltered behind the leader but Frank, with the lightest bike and the strongest legs, pulled ahead so that we each had to carve our furrow through the wind. We buttoned down the cuffs and closed up flapping collars. We pulled our caps around so that the peaks pointed to the rear and still Frank was a hundred yards ahead.

I had wanted to take a different route on the return to Bapaume but I could not get near enough to Frank to make myself heard. I had found a road on the map which cut across the wind which would lessen our effort but he ground on ahead of us and we had to follow. I cursed the wind, I cursed Frank, I cursed my stupidity. I broke into my emergency rations and morosely munched my way, square by square through a bar of black chocolate. Towards the end of the journey I was convinced that I could actually feel the energy produced as I ate each square.

We got back to the hotel and went with the minimum of fuss to our rooms. In the dining room that night we were quite subdued.

'What was today's mileage?' Frank asked.

We ate some paté.

'One hundred and eight miles,' I said.

We ate some more.

Hairy said, 'That's a lot of miles.'

'Too many really,' I admitted.

'Not your fault. We would have been alright except for that wind,' Frank said and then he astonished us by the candid and quite unexpected disclosure, 'I think the serving girl is smashing, don't you? Lovely figure.'

I didn't know what to say. I almost doubted that I had

heard it. Frank had never made any such allusions in all the time that I had known him. He was not that sort of person. When mates nudged each other in the ribs and winked, he always remained aloof from any such behaviour. I could not understand why he had broken the unwritten custom that us three blokes did not talk about sex and women when we were cycling. We didn't flirt, we never even looked at a woman. We just enjoyed the cycling.

I was shocked, not only that he had expressed the opinion but that this revealed his having made the initial assessment. Frank! Of all people. He didn't do that sort of thing. But I think what surprised me most of all was that he found the serving girl attractive when, seated behind him was a really hot bit of stuff in a flame red dress and searing black eyes, olive skin and sparkling teeth. Compared to the rather plain waitress that he fancied, she was as velvet is to cotton, but I suppose he could not see her from where he was sitting. Even I had been obliged to lean out quite a way from my seat and look in the mirror above the aquarium.

chapter fifteen

In any narrative, a repeated use of the declaration, 'I woke up in the morning,' will inevitably call up visions of a drawling blues singer so I shall avoid such a possibility by starting at lunch. We ate at the British Cemetery outside Avesnes le Comte. It was the first military cemetery the other two had visited. I had not pressed it upon them; I made no lofty speeches; I did not philosophise. I know not what went on in their heads but it appeared that their first visit affected them as much as my first visit had affected me.

As if to rub the lesson home, several miles further on I showed them the corner of a field which the farmer had left unaltered since the end of the First World War. This was his tribute to the glorious fallen. It was sobering to watch the cows stagger, grumbling up and down the shell torn hillocks whilst the wind ruffled the sparse grass.

But what we needed was enervation. The previous day's mileage had taken its toll of our physical reserves; the disagreements had done likewise to our mental stock. The continuous nagging and tugging which the breeze had subjected us to throughout the morning had not uplifted our spirits. Cycling across the open plains of the Artois against the lucid and persistent argument of the wind was the last thing that we needed.

We arrived at the small town of St. Pol sur Ternoise in the early afternoon and for once they did not argue when I said that we would stop cycling for the day. We unbuckled bags, washed and changed and then set out to do the town.

It was dead. In St. Pol sur Ternoise it is early closing day every day. Even the charming young lady sitting in the Syndicat d'Initiative, rather than dispense us some tourist information, exuded a boredom and looked at her wrist-watch whilst we were talking to her. The trains rumbled through the station, the newspapers flapped listlessly on the news stand. There was nothing to do.

Hairy came up with a brilliant idea.

'Let's find a bar and get drunk.'

Terrific.

I bought a paperback book at the Maison de la Presse and said, 'I don't mind what you do, I'm going back to the hotel to do a spot of reading.'

What an admission of ennui – lying on the bed and reading. It was what guests did to fill in the time before dinner when staying with friends.

Hairy and Frank went off to get drunk. An hour later they came back, bounding up the stairs like late choirboys.

'Hey we've found a terrific bar!'

'You don't say.'

'You've gotta come and have a look. It's not the kind of bar you would expect to find here.'

'That I can imagine.'

'Come on. Get your shoes on. Take your anorak – it's just spitting a little.'

'Oh, glorious.'

With a deal of obvious bad grace, I sloshed a zig-zag course across the puddle-patched car park towards the pink neon sign. The only pink neon sign in the whole of St. Pol.

'Apart from the beer of course...'

'Of course.'

'...they've got a pool table. French pool.'

'Oh goody.'

'And instead of having the holes set right back in the cushions, they are flat on the table.'

'Wow.'

My sarcasm was not getting through to them which made me even more grumpy.

Crossing the threshold of the bar was the nearest I have come to stepping into another world. Outside, St. Pol was dark, damp and dead. Inside, it was sparkling with light and thrumming with energy. At the far end of the bar, three men were playing a boisterous game of *quatre cents vingt-et-un*. Wreathed in genies of blue cigarette smoke, they lobbed dice into the tray, shouting and arguing over every score. In one corner, a handful of girls were gyrating before a glowing juke box. To the rhythm of the music was added the syncopated clopping of a ping pong ball although for the life of me I could not see where the game was being played.

'Hello fellers!' The barman seemed to be on intimate terms with Frank and Hairy which I took to be a bad omen. They acknowledged his salutation regally.

'What would you like to drink?' Hairy asked me. I suppose he felt a bit guilty.

'I'll have a San Pellegrino.'

'A what?'

'A San Pellegrino. Ask your mate, the barman. He'll know what I want.'

Frank moved towards the pool table apologetically.

'I'll set the balls up.'

'Good idea, ' Hairy acquiesced and then turned to me, 'Err... I don't think the barman understands my French. What is a San Pellegrino?'

'It's like an aromatic bitters. Comes in a thin tapering bottle.'

'Can't you have a lemonade?'

'Oh alright. I'll have a bottle of Sic.'

'He says he hasn't got any Sic will Pschitt do instead?'

'Admirably.'

'Good. Do you... fancy a game of pool?'

'I'll watch you two play.'

Frank's normal game of pool is played with immense

165

energy and approximate accuracy, the one, complementing the other to produce unfairly creditable results. Hairy's game is scientific, serious and methodical. And he always loses. Unfortunately for Frank, the different configuration of the French table did not happily accept his ungentle élan. His first cannonball shot bounced from the slate and roared through a nearby game of dominoes like a stolen Ford Capri through a shopping precinct. It ended up smack against the wall under the juke box.

Whilst Frank was retrieving the ball, a surprisingly long operation involving crawling about at ankle height amongst the mini-skirted girls, one of the domino players rose sedately from his table and, mistakenly believing Hairy to have been the vandal, patiently and with good humour, gave him a lesson in gentle pool playing.

It was going to be a long night. I hate contests at the best of times and this was one of the worst of times. Everywhere that I looked, games were being joined, fought over and applauded: table tennis out the back somewhere, dominoes down here, pool over there in the middle, dice cavorting around the felt tray on the bar. The posters pinned to the wall announced 'Concours de Pétanque' and 'Match de Football.' The glass shelves behind the bar were groaning with cups, shields, trophies and rosettes. Even the television showed the wobbly black and white image of some youngsters ten-pin bowling. I blinked. I knew one of them. The one with the funny cap and the moustache. I didn't know his name but I knew I had seen his face.

'Frank, Hairy, come and have a look at this.'

'Just a minute.'

'It's only ten-pin bowling. Boring.'

'No, come on. Look at that bloke on the telly doing the bowling. I'm sure I've seen him before. I don't know who he is but I'm sure of it.'

Frank and Hairy were clearly bored with the screen. They could at least have been a little grateful for the fact that I was now no longer sulking. I was almost displaying a sort of interest in their café full of games.

Frank looked at Hairy and then admitted, 'Yes I've seen him before as well. And so has Hairy.'

'I thought so. I thought so. Where have we seen him?'

Frank moved his gaze blandly from me to the screen again. The image was a bit fuzzy and it was unusual to find a black and white television in a bar – they usually installed colour sets. I began to feel a misgiving which was not settled in any way by Frank beckoning me. I followed him around the bar, past the dominoes, alongside the ping-pong table and through a doorway where he silently showed me the five-lane bowling alley and the man in the funny cap.

'It's closed circuit television.' He pointed at the camera. 'The picture goes down that wire to–'

'All right Clever Clogs, I know how it works.'

He said no more but pulled what I thought was a very rude face. When we got back to the front of the bar, Hairy was well into an Anglo-French pool challenge. His opponent was, we assumed, the café champion. Every time he bent over the table his little brown leather jacket sprung above his belt and pulled his shirt up. And every time he straightened up he tucked the shirt back in again.

Frank graciously offered to annihilate the upstart opposition for the honour of the team

'Do you want me to finish him off?'

'Under the juke-box or on the domino table?' Hairy retorted, not without justification, I thought.

Actually, Hairy was doing very well. His meticulous technique and scientific approach was exactly what this table needed. His ball would roll to the lip and just totter in whereas if Frank had played the shot, the ball would have gone through the window and down the street, pole-axing three passing nuns on the way.

The men playing dice suspended their game and sauntered over. Plop! Another ball went down.

'He's two balls ahead Hairy. Shall I jog his elbow?' Frank suggested.

A French man with a wart, hearing this foreign aside, handed the chalk to Hairy with a gruff, '*Bitteschoen*.'

'*Danke schoen*,' Hairy replied automatically.

Wartface nodded knowingly at the others in the café.

'*Des Allemands*,' he announced. '*Je m'en doutais*.'

I warned Hairy. 'They think we're Krauts.'

'Oh brilliant!' he muttered. 'That is all I can say in German.'

'Look out Hairy, the cue-ball's going down!' Frank shouted. 'Get the spoon!'

This strange exhortation made little sense to me but, miraculously, a teaspoon appeared from over the bar and was plunged into the hole alongside the cue ball, wedging it in position. For reasons only known to himself, Frank, our only fluent German speaker, said,

'*Gracias senor*,' in perfect Spanish.

Wartface modified his opinion,

'*Merde! Des Espingouins!*'

One of the others muttered what I took to be the equivalent of, 'We'll soon see about that' and then hailed a certain 'Yako' at the back of the bar.

Yako was propelled forward. He was a swarthy man with black hair and no doubt a penchant for waving red tablecloths at bulls. There was no way that we would be able to fool him. Nearly knocking me flat with his halitosis, he questioned me in rapid bubbling Spanish, spraying me with a fine coating of saliva as he did so. I recalled the one, frantic term of colloquial Dutch studies that I had completed at college and replied.

'*De tafel is in het midden van de eetkamer*.'

'*Que?*' He looked around him, fearful of losing his credibility as a Bona Fide Iberian.

'*Wie eet pape?*' I asked him, although I could hardly expect him to know who was eating porridge.

He drew himself up to his full height of five foot three inches, gazed around him with increasing confidence and decreed in a voice turgid with scorn, '*Des Russes.*'

Derisive laughter greeted this announcement and he retired in ignominy. During the ensuing uproar, Hairy irretrievably potted the cue-ball when no spoon was to hand, thus losing us one of the games that we were playing but the other was not yet settled. From the back of the jubilant and noisy crowd was thrown the tentative query, 'Rushki?'

'*Pravilna!*' Frank replied without looking up.

'What the hell does that mean?' I hissed at him.

'"Naturally". It's Russian. I once drank vodka with the captain of a Russian whaler in Liverpool.'

'Do you know any more?'

'Not a word.'

Luckily our challenger appeared unwilling to test his knowledge of the language either, so Russian we remained.

'Come on you chaps! Some vodka for the Russians.' The barman majestically laid out three miniscule glasses onto the bar and tipped a finger of vodka into each. 'Kameraden,' he invited us.

'I can't drink vodka – it's alcohol,' I whispered to Frank. 'Do something. Tell him I'm a teetotaler or Ukrainian or something.'

Hairy picked up his glass and knocked back the liquid in one gulp. He didn't speak again until we were on our way back to the hotel. Frank pointed at me and apologetically slid my glass back to the barman.

'Moscovitch Lada Polski-Fiat Pravda,' he explained.

The barman turned a sad and indulgent eye upon me and drained the glass himself. The crowd cheered and clapped. The barman, overtaken with enthusiasm, tossed the glass over his shoulder where it bounced unbroken off the ice bucket. The evening had all the makings of quite a party, a party in which I did not particularly want to take part. Time to start moving. Hairy was going red in the face from holding his breath so I took hold of his elbow and began to steer him towards the door. Frank covered our tactical withdrawal with a raised clenched fist and a 'Dostoievsky Vladivostock.'

Sitting alone on a stool by the door with an incongruous glass of red wine set before him, was a man of Indian race. He was probably a Mauritian hotel porter or a Malagasy road sweeper. It was too tempting. It was too fortuitous to ignore. As his brown fingers closed hesitantly around the stem of the glass, I pronounced clearly,

'*Bachate raho mai se dama-i-taqwa, na lag jae dhoba kahin is najis ka.*'

He dropped the glass as if it had been electrified and as we passed into the damp night shroud, I could hear his plaintive but ignored voice trilling, 'Your Russians speak Hindustani,' then the door closed.

'Well... they beat us at pool,' Frank summed up. 'What did you say to Gunga Din on the way out?'

'Oh, just a little Hindu expression that I learned some time ago.'

'Oh yeah. What did it mean?'

'"Save your skirt of piety from the defiling touch of spirituous liquors lest it be polluted by this unholy thing."'

'I think that makes the score one all.'

With a burst of expelled breath, Hairy warned us vehemently, 'I'm not going back for a tie-breaker match.'

chapter sixteen

'Really we are just going home now, aren't we?' Frank observed with a tinge of sadness in his voice.

I replied quite honestly.

'Well I suppose we are, but I always try to make it more interesting than just a return journey.' At that very moment Hairy crashed with a grunt into a pothole. 'Mind the pothole,' I added.

'If this is what you call "more interesting" then I can cope with the mundane,' he grumbled. 'Where are we having lunch?'

'Where we like. As long as we end up at St.Omer tonight, we can stop where it pleases us – we have our picnic with us.'

'Don't forget we've got no bread.'

'We'll get some,' I assured them.

'When?'

'At about eleven o'clock.'

'Where?'

'From the bread van.'

They exchanged glances and Frank began to whistle

between his teeth. We were heading westward out of St. Pol into a brisk breeze which I blamed for their fractiousness. The sky was overcast and the clouds were rolling ominously close to the gentle rounded hills through which we would shortly be pedalling.

'We'll soon be turning north and we'll get out of this wind.' I tried to encourage them.

'I hope you've told the bread van.'

The climb northwards from the valley of the Ternoise towards the valley of the Lys was gentle but persistent. It brought us out on the top of a bald plateau, sprinkled with silent farms. A forgotten land where nobody went. From every road junction parted at least one unmade, flinty track leading to nowhere. Generations ago somebody must have travelled along these old ways but now they represented the abandoned tentacles of some high level network of long distance pathways.

I braved Frank's displeasure and chose one of these tracks, explaining that it would save us a couple of miles. We bumped and rattled along a field edge which was cunningly hugging the invisible contour line. Around the side of the hill we found a ruined and empty stone house, nettles growing higher than the remains of the walls. We looked at it, not speaking, and continued our way till we joined the metalled road once again at another junction. I looked back up the track curving gently out of sight. With its crumbling chalk edges and scrubby spine of tufty grass, it looked just the same as the other end. For all we knew we could have been travelling in the opposite direction. It was a palindrome of a path.

Frank spoke for all of us. 'This place gives me the willies.'

I held up my finger for silence. I had heard the repeated shrieking of a motor horn. I quickly unfolded the map and located the nearest village in the direction whence the sound had issued.

'Come on,' I said. 'We'll have to go down here and get some bread.'

'What about–?'

'Don't argue, just follow me.'

Mystified and intrigued, they followed me off the plateau, slithering down a chute of a track. We slipped into the hamlet by the road alongside the church. A patchy dog had been trotting across the otherwise deserted square. Seeing us, he veered towards us and then stopped and watched. Slowly, one hind leg crept up on him and scratched him violently behind the ear. He threw up his nose and sniffed twice, released one sharp bark and then trotted off.

'Some guard dog!' Frank observed.

'Careful, it could be a trap,' Hairy loved his ration of melodrama.

'You mean it could be a decoy?'

'Don't be daft that wasn't a decoy, it was a wire terrier.'

'Looked more like a wire brush to me.'

'Not wire brush but why're we here?'

Toot toot.

'I told you. To buy some bread.'

'Where from?'

Toot toot.

'Just be patient. I've not failed you yet have I?'

'Well now you come to mention it, you were wrong about the battle of Crécy.'

Toot toot.

'Only in minor details.'

'You didn't mention that it rained during the battle.'

'It's unlucky to mention rain when you are cycling.'

Toot toot.

'That makes it worse. You never even mentioned that they fought the battle on bicycles.'

'Don't be obtuse. Come on, let's get the bread.'

Into the square lurched a bumptious white van and

through its windows peeked the summits of a Himalayan range of golden loaves.

Toot toot. The horn was utterly incongruous. It was the panic shrieking of a forty foot long articulated lorry as it slithered on a greasy road towards the bus queue; it was the bullying bellow of an arrogant Mercedes open top tourer as it scoured around an alpine pass. It was not at all the sound that one would have normally associated with this clod of a vehicle. Frank was scandalised.

'Do you mean to say that it was that poxy little paper bag making all that noise?'

'Sounds worse than tortured cats.'

'When did you last torture a cat?'

'Don't start you two! It's the bread van, whether you like it or not.'

'How did you know it would be here?'

'Easy peasy. It's marked on the map.'

'Oh.' Hairy thought for a moment. 'Just a minute...'

But we were already scooting down the square to buy bread.

It must have been the lunch stop which recharged Hairy's battery. As we resumed the climb up the dry valley, an apparition like dracula on wheels, swooped down a steep side road behind us and with the momentum gained from such a vertiginous descent, shot past us as if our tyres had been concrete. I turned to pull a facetious face at Frank but he snapped his fingers, pointed at the flying ragbag and uttered the immortal words,

'After her Hairy!'

'Right.'

Hairy set his chin to a determined angle, waggled a few levers on his bike and churned off in pursuit.

'Go it Hairy!'

'You can do it!'

The woman turned a pasty witch-like face and espied Hairy bearing down upon her with all his gadgets working;

from the echo-sounder on his helmet to the radar scanner on his crossbar. It could not have been a pretty sight.

'Good God, she's pulling away from him.'

'Come on Hairy, best pedal downwards!'

We reached a side road.

'I think we turn off here,' I said to Frank and we stopped to watch the old lady, raincoat cracking like a spinnaker, holding grimly to her lead.

'Do you think we ought to call him back?'

We watched some more.

'Be against the rules, wouldn't it?'

'S'pose so.'

We looked up the road.

'He's nearly caught her. Better wait a bit.'

'Yes... he wouldn't thank us for recalling him when he was just on the point of victory would he?'

'No I suppose not.'

We watched the two figures becoming smaller.

'Hmm. Hope he gets her before they go out of sight.'

'Yeah. Could be awkward couldn't it?'

Luckily, Hairy had remained in full knowledge of the developments by means of his rear view mirror, or was it his satellite tracking system? Anyhow, as soon as he had raised his arm to signal that he had passed her, he veered around and hustled back down the hill to a hero's welcome. As a piece of utterly pointless cycling it had no equal.

'The old biddy said something to me as I passed her. I don't think she was very pleased,' he announced.

'What did she say?'

Hairy repeated the phrase as best he could. Even his approximation of the guttural exclamation was enough for me to recognise such a distinctive oath.

'No, she was not very pleased.' I concurred.

'Was it rude?'

'Very rude'

'Very very rude?'

'No, just very rude. You would never use it.'

'I see... What did you two stop for? Was I going too fast?'

'That'll be the day.'

I nodded at the sign. 'We have to turn off here.'

Hairy read, 'Pale Fart.'

'It is pronounced *palfar*.'

'It's spelt "pale fart" isn't it Frank?'

'Indubitably.'

'Right then, Pale Fart it is.'

I didn't argue, after all, he was our champion for the day.

I had a treat in store for Hairy. That afternoon we were due to stop at the town of Arques. Before the motorway was built you might have driven through Arques on your way from Calais to Paris. I did. Somehow it always seemed to be at night. Up the main street I would crawl, bumping over the incorrectly named level crossings and passing under the black, shadowy gantries which stretched from building to building to permit the personnel from the glass works to cross the road in safety. Through gateways in the factory wall I would glimpse silhouette figures loading packaged glassware into waiting lorries, the whole scene lit by discreet orange and yellow glows which seeped from the different doorways and ventilators.

Once, when returning across country towards Calais, I was met by a sight which I can remember vividly to this day. It was about ten o'clock at night and I was driving along an undulating, tree-lined road. An occasional vehicle would pass in the opposite direction but the last one had been at least five minutes earlier.

Then, in the far distance, a pair of yellow headlights flickered over the crest of the hill, only to be cut from view as my section of the road descended into a dip. When I breasted the rise, I saw that the headlights had doubled. Then there were more and then, to my enchantment, over the hills and around the corners two miles ahead of me writhed a sparkling yellow serpent. A liquid stream of golden lava flowing over the ground towards me. Closer and closer it came until fifty six cars went past in the opposite direction, nose to tail. I counted them. To have seen three cars together at that time of night would have been an event, but fifty six! It took my breath away and then I wondered if some dreadful event had occurred and they were all fleeing the town ahead of me, for there was no vehicle travelling in my direction. When I entered the next town would I find it in the terror-stricken grip of a giant dinosaur or a fleet of martians? The explanation, when it came, was far less frightening. The shimmering necklace was only the night shift turning in to work at the glass works at Arques.

So I was leading Hairy to Arques for a treat but it had nothing to do with glass factories. Arques is a town which is squeezed untidily into the junction of valleys of the rivers Lys and Aa. The latter being a favourite of French crossword puzzle compilers. To the west of Arques, the hills of the Boulonnais region dominate the skyline whilst travelling northwards brings the traveller onto the undulating land which soon degenerates into the canal-strewn handkerchief of Belgian Flanders.

The north of France and the south of Belgium are well served by canals. The land is ideal, for it is extensively flat and historically the demand for canals was there to transport the coals dug from the northern coalfields. When I talk of canals, you must not conjure up in your mind a green, weed-choked ditch meandering prettily between bankside pubs and shops with an occasional brightly painted balance bridge plonked artistically across it for aesthetic effect.

The canals of France start at Calais with the Calais to St. Omer Canal, wider than a motorway and just as busy. The boats which travel along it have the same relationship to our English narrow boats as the modern TIR trucks do to the dainty little lorries of the 1950s. Moving southwards, these canals link the great river valleys – the Somme, the Oise, the Seine – into a network which is so comprehensive that it is possible to go in to France at Calais and come out at the Mediterranean.

However, this is rather straying from the point. The importance of Arques in this system is that this is where the *Canal du Neuffossé* met the *Canal de Calais à St. Omer*. Unfortunately there was a forty foot height difference between the two canal levels. Standard canal practice was followed and a flight of five locks was built but the French engineers looked for an improvement to permit faster operation.

And they looked to that bastion of nineteenth century industry, Great Britain, and constructed a canal lift to replace the locks. It was a cathedral of orange brick towers and green cast iron. It functioned in this manner. The boat coming down the canal would run into an enormous trough. Forty feet below it, the boat wishing to move up the canal would do the same. When both boats were tied up and the locks closed, the top trough would descend vertically to the level of the canal below whilst the bottom trough rose to the canal above. The system worked by a hydraulic balance pushing two enormous pistons, one under each trough.

It was built in 1887 and functioned for eighty years and no matter what it says in the guide book, and despite what the bargees may try to convince you of the *génie* in French engineering, the maker's name plate stands proud and clear and to this day. And it is British.

We had some trouble reaching the *Ascenseur des Fontinettes* as it is called. It was, quite naturally, built to be accessible from the canal and we were stupidly trying to reach it by road. I had thought that I knew where it was.

'It must be this way.'

They dutifully churned around a ploughed field and expressed no surprise whatsoever when we landed up on the cracked and overgrown concrete perimeter road of a long-abandoned airfield.

I mused aloud. 'I wonder if this is the former St. Omer fighter airfield?'

Frank ignored my remark but turned to Hairy and said, 'I knew it. I knew he was leading you on. This was what he came to see really. Some obscure acres of crumbling concrete. I never believed his story about canals in the first place. When did you last see a canal on top of a hill?'

'Last March in the Pennines.'

'He's probably going to tell us some story about this being the field that the first world war RFC ace, Mick Mc. Cudden crashed in.'

'How did you know about Mc. Cudden?' I asked.

'You're not the only one to read books, you know.'

'I wasn't going to mention Mc. Cudden.'

'That's alright then. What about Douglas Bader?'

'What about Douglas Bader?'

'Aren't you going to mention him?'

'Why?'

'Well after he was captured, the RAF parachuted his spare artificial leg on to St. Omer aerodrome for him, didn't they?'

'Did they? Why?'

'Because the Germans were holding him in St. Omer hospital.'

'Oh yes.'

'Before he escaped by climbing down three knotted sheets, of course.'

'Ah, I knew about that bit. I saw the film.'

Hairy had been following this opportunist challenge to my omniscience with amused interest. Whatever the result, he would gain by it. He looked down at the scrubby grass poking through the gaps in the concrete road and said,

'And all this happened here on this aerodrome?'

He looked at me for confirmation. I glanced at Frank. Frank scratched his upper lip.

I committed myself. 'Yes, that's right. Of course I was going to introduce it at some stage in the day–'

'Thought so,' Frank muttered.

'–but now that we are here on the actual spot...'

Frank cleared his throat. 'Not quite,' he said. 'St. Omer aerodrome is about two miles to our west, over by those trees.' He pointed to a dark smudge. 'Where that Piper Commanche has just taken off from.'

I was not accepting that. There was no way that he could discern the model of the plane from that distance. My scorn was scorching.

'How can you see what type of plane it is from here?'

'Listen Sunshine... you couldn't even see the blessed aerodrome.'

We found the canal lift and the fountain of their wonderment soon scoured the dregs of dissatisfaction from the aquifer of their curiosity. We followed the elderly guide as he stumped about the structure, pointing to various bits of machinery. When he spoke, he applied great precision to forming his lips into the appropriate shape and drawing in just the correct amount of breath to be expelled through his larynx in order that his utterances might be perfectly modulated. It was a great shame that we could not understand a word that he said. We never did discover what language he was speaking. Perhaps our fame had preceded us and he already knew that we were Russian. It was a shame but no more. We did not need him. The *Ascenseur des Fontinettes* speaks for itself.

Our bedroom in the hotel in St. Omer had three beds and three windows. Two looked down the main street and the other across the square, through the tree tops of which we could glimpse the luxurious and expensive hotel which we could not afford to even spit at. Our lodging place was not only cheap, it was sordid and squalid. The door would not close properly, the beds were frail and the state of the toilet down the corridor was obscene. Indeed the only factor to be counted in the toilet's favour was its location. From this distance we were spared most of the stench and the encroaching fluids.

At that moment I vowed to myself that one day I would do this type of trip again and I would spend money. There was no reason why possession of a bicycle should so inhibit me that I would accept such filth and degradation. Why should I? No more sardines and truckle beds, next time it would be all lobster and four-posters.

It was going to be our last night in France. Tomorrow we would be in Calais. The rain clouds were retreating fluffy grey over the western horizon as, on the rain-washed pavement outside the pizza restaurant, we debated our forthcoming evening.

'Let's go to the bar across the road.'

'Good idea.'

'You two go. I thought I might just take a walk. Have a look around the town.'

Even on our last evening, I could not bend. I could make no effort to bridge the rift we had tried to ignore but which existed between us. We went our separate ways. That last night in St. Omer, Frank and Hairy got thrown out of a bar but have never told me why and I was whistled at by three girls for a reason I would not wish to divulge.

The air was clear, cool and almost Spring like on the morrow. With no pangs of regret we bade a hearty *adieu*, not an *au revoir* but an unequivocal *adieu* to our overnight stop. We would not be returning there. Ever.

We stood on the pavement, cuddling our bicycles and trying to decide how to find the canal which would lead us to Calais. An English car nosed its bonnet elegantly through the gateway of the four star hotel opposite. It paused for an instant and then wallowed into the street. As it passed I heard a phrase spoken on the radio. Frank saw my puzzled face.

'What's the matter?'

'Did you hear what the announcer said on Radio 3?'

'I don't listen to Radio 3.'

'No, I mean just now, when that car went past. They had the radio on.'

'And?'

'The announcer said, "Goethe was paid in duck eggs."'

'That's why I don't listen to Radio 3. They say some daft things on it.'

We mounted our bicycles and rode to Calais.

I was sitting in my study and silently watching the cold winter rain drizzling down the window pane. The trees were glistening black skeletons, the sea, a bland grey. I had just come across the folder containing the sketches I had made on my cycle trips. I had laid them out on my desk before me. They were sunshine.

The telephone rang but I did not want to answer it. I was seeing France from my handlebars. It kept ringing.

I picked up the receiver. It was Frank. 'Ducats,' he said.

'What?'

'St. Omer. Last summer. That awful hotel.'

'Yes?'

'We were standing outside on the last morning and you heard something on a car radio.'

'Yes?'

I remembered vaguely. I was astonished that he had any recollection of it.

'Well it was ducats,' he said. 'Goethe was paid in ducats not duck eggs. I checked with the BBC.'

'You did what?'

'Well, I knew it would worry you.' He sounded a little embarrassed.

'Oh.'

'So when are we going back to France?'

'Funny you should say that...'

I pulled down my box of IGN maps

ILLUSTRATIONS

'Bilbao? In Portugal?'

I was flabbergasted.

'No, Bilbao in Spain. It's not in Portugal.'

He had always been fairly hot on geography but I did not see that quality as a justification for his moving to Bilbao, wherever he claimed it to be.

'But why do you want to go to Bilbao?'

'I'm marrying a Spanish girl,' he said.

'Congratulations, or whatever it is in Spanish.'

He said something foreign that sounded strangely like *'Felix the Cat'*

'Why don't you come and stay?' he added.

I considered his generosity to be a bit excessive. Indeed, it bordered on the reckless.

'What about your 'intended'?' I asked.

'She's listening on the other phone.' Good job he told me that. 'I thought that you could bring your bicycle. They do a lot of cycling around here.'

'Well...'

'Ah, go on. Look at all the trouble you have had with France over the years. You wouldn't have any of those problems here.'

'What trouble?' I suddenly felt defensive of France's reputation.

'Well what about that momentous day when you locked your bicycle to the front of Boulogne railway station and then remembered that you had left the key to your padlock on your bedside table – in England?'

'That was just forgetfulness on my part. You can't blame France for that.'

'You did. And what about that trip where they dug the road up for two kilometres and left you wading through ankle deep clay in the pouring rain? You were not too enamoured with France then.'

'I got over it.'

'You had to throw away your shoes.'

'They were nearly worn out anyway.'

'And cycling down the motorway at Valenciennes? That wasn't too clever was it?'

'It was Sunday morning.'

'It was still a motorway.'

'I misread the sign. It can happen to anybody.'

'But the point is, it happened to you. By the way, I never did hear how you got out of that one.'

'I had to lift my bicycle over the crash barrier, slide down the embankment and then clamber over the fence at the bottom.'

'Not an easy thing to do with a loaded touring bicycle I should imagine. You didn't get caught by the police then?'

'Yes, I did get caught.'

'What did they say?'

'"Lift your bike over the barrier, slide down the bank and climb over the fence at the bottom".'

'Quite pragmatic, the French, aren't they? And have you quite forgotten the rain?'

He was like a terrier with a rat.

'Everywhere has rain.'

'You got so wet that the dye ran out of your trousers and stained your feet blue.'

'That was the fault of the trousers.'

'Well you won't have any of those sort of problems in Spain. The sun shines, the food is great and the hotels are cheap. And the colours are fast.'

'So is the traffic from what I hear.'

'Not where I am going. It's rustic somnolence. Think about it.'

And I did.

The Trouble With Spain has now been published.

a cycle safari through France

Hunting
the Golden
Lion

Martin Lloyd

Hunting
the
Golden Lion

a cycle safari through France

Having recklessly declared in a previous book that it
must be possible to cross all of France staying only
in hotels called the HOTEL DU LION D'OR,
Martin Lloyd is challenged by his critics to prove
his assertion in the only way possible – by doing it.

Surely it will be a straightforward and leisurely ride
through France? As long as the hotels are no more than
a day's cycle ride apart, of course. And if your bicycle
has been constructed this century, and if you remember
to take with you all that you need... and if your name isn't
Martin Lloyd.

Is this why, on the the first day of his safari,
he is standing in his pyjamas on a pavement
a thousand miles from home,
clutching a broken bicycle
with a bleeding hand?

Published by Queen Anne's Fan ISBN: 9780 9547 1506 9

The Trouble with Spain

MARTIN LLOYD

FROM THE BESTSELLING AUTHOR OF
THE TROUBLE WITH FRANCE *COMES*
THIS EAGERLY AWAITED SEQUEL

'*...makes Munchausen look like a liar...*'

Still smarting from his brutal encounter with Gaul as detailed in his much acclaimed book, THE TROUBLE WITH FRANCE, Martin Lloyd drags his bicycle over the Pyrenees to pursue the twin delights of sun and breakfast.

What factor will defeat his proposed headlong plunge into raw hedonism? Will it be his profound and extensive ignorance of Spanish history or perhaps his coarse insensitivity to the culture of the peninsula?
Or would it be the damning condemnation that he is just too lazy to learn the language?

Read THE TROUBLE WITH SPAIN and you will discover nothing about bull fights and enjoy no colourful descriptions of sensual flamenco dancing but you will learn why you cannot train goldfish to be guard dogs and you will clearly understand why even Martin Lloyd's trousers ran away from him.

CAUTION
This book contains moderate use of humour, some expressions in foreign language and a short but ultimately frustrating scene in a lady's bedroom.

The Chinese Transfer

The Chinese Transfer

a thriller romance that you will
not want to put down

'...this is storytelling as it used to be...'

Paris in the 1970s – student demonstrations, union
strikes and oppressive heat. Coach driver Simon
Laperche is sent to Orly Airport to pick up a Chinese
group and take them to their hotel in the city. A run
of the mill job. He could do it with his eyes shut.
It was a pity about the guide, but then, he could
not expect to please everybody.

Abruptly, things go wrong. The plane is diverted to
Lyons and Laperche is ordered to drive his coach
south to meet it... and he has to take that infuriating
guide with him. Unknown to them both,
a terrorist unit has targeted their group and
is intent upon its destruction.

Stalked by the terrorists, the driver and guide continue
to bicker as they struggle to bring their group safely to
Paris. Will the mutual respect which eventually begins
to grow between them prove strong enough
when the test comes?

Published by Queen Anne's Fan ISBN: 9780 9547 15021

Rue Amélie

Rue Amélie

Martin Lloyd

another fast-paced thriller from Martin Lloyd.

Following the success of *The Chinese Transfer,* Martin Lloyd takes us back to the seedy side of Paris in the 1970s. Joel LeBatard, a driver for a small-time crook, loses his boss's car and his position. With no job and soon to be thrown out of his bedsit, he accepts a commission from a woman he meets at a funeral, to find out where her father had invested his secret pension.

LeBatard discovers that others are on the same trail – a ruthless big-time gangster whom he has already been stupid enough to upset, and an ex-colleague from his army days who now heads an undercover squad in the Ministry of Defence. They will stop at nothing to get their hands on the very thing that he is looking for, but nobody can tell him what it is.

The hectic action takes them to the four corners of Paris. Whilst pursuing his relentless search, LeBatard struggles with two difficulties: is his new employer telling him the truth and how, in the face of such energy and charm, can he uphold his vow never to get mixed up with another woman?

Published by Queen Anne's Fan ISBN: 9780 9547 1507 6

The Impetus Turn

In the 1980's a civil engineer is sent to work
in Bangladesh and is thrown into a world
of stark contrasts; of povery and disease,
of diplomatic parties, corporate power
and corruption.

With a naivety aggravated by his stubbornness,
he begins to uncover a fraud which threatens
to cause devastating repercussions in the
political arena and exert a disastrous
influence upon his career.

Should he continue?

Published by Queen Anne's Fan ISBN: 9780 9573 639-5-3

Every Picture

'... a tender and engaging love story...'

When the son of an earl meets the daughter of
a coal miner in the doorway of the art college he
does not tell her that he is a viscount.

Why should he?

How was he to know that their paths would cross
and recross and that he would fall in
love with her?

And once that has happened, he finds it impossible to
tell her the truth for fear of losing her. At the very
moment that they finally admit their feelings for one
another, the relationship is wrenched asunder as their
lives take a violent and unpredictable turn, casting their
two destinies onto divergent courses.

Will they ever meet again?

Published by Queen Anne's Fan ISBN: 9780 9547 1505 2

THE PASSPORT

*The History of Man's Most
Travelled Document*
by Martin Lloyd
SECOND EDITION, REVISED
AND ENLARGED WITH
246 pages 80 illustrations

The passport is a document familiar to many, used
and recognised worldwide and yet it has no basis in
law: one country cannot oblige another to admit its
subjects simply by issuing a document. But the state,
by insisting on the requirement to hold a passport,
provides for itself a neat, self-financing data collection
and surveillance system. This well illustrated book
tells for the first time the story of the passport from
its earliest origins to its latest high-tech developments.
Handwritten documents adorned with wax seals,
modern versions in plastic covers, diplomatic
passports and wartime safe conducts, all drawn
from the author's collection, complement the
exciting exploits of spies and criminals.

Whether recounting the birth of the British blue
passport of the 1920s or divulging the secrets of
today's machine readable passport, Martin Lloyd has
written an informative and engrossing history book
which is accessible to everyone.

'...a lively and thoughtful book...'
SUNDAY TELEGRAPH

Published by Queen Anne's Fan ISBN: 9780 9547 1503 8